[Document title]

My Years at Sea

By Theodore Pitsios

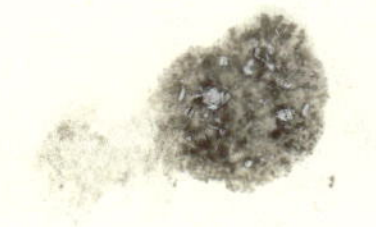

This is a nonfiction biography by
Theodore Pitsios

Published by
Doctor's Dreams Publishing
Biloxi, MS

Printed in the United States of America
ICBN: 978-1-942181-58-3

Author's Bio:

Theodore Pitsios was born in the village of Tsagarade, Greece. After graduating from the Maritime Academy in 1961, he sailed as an engineer in the merchant marine for a number of years. Before settling in the US Gulf Coast, he lived in Nassau, Bahamas, and in West Palm Beach, Florida. When not traveling, he divides his time between his homes in Greece and in Orange Beach, Alabama.

Previous works by the author:

The Bellmaker's House
Searching for Ithica
Walking in the Light
The First Half of My Life

Cover Drawing: Dimitra Pitsios

CHAPTER ONE

I know I'd look much better if I said that all the good things that happened in my life were the result of careful planning and prudent thinking, but it wouldn't be the truth, and starting with a lie would give the whole story the believability of an old mariner's yarn which would be a shame because every bit of the writing in here is true.

For instance, my choice to become an engineer in the merchant marine: Looking back, I think it was Providence that arranged it to happen this way. In my village, most of the boys my age, when asked what they would like to be when they grew up, the first answer was a *voithos sto leoforio* (a helper on the bus). At that time, we considered it to be what my grandchildren now would call *a cool* job.

The bus that connected our village with the world beyond the mountain came by twice a day: early in the morning on the way to Volos and returned from there early in the evening. The *voithos* was the one who received the luggage from the passengers and stowed it on top of the bus. He also got to ride on the bus's doorstep while the bus was moving after he had removed the rock from the rear wheel and did many other *cool* things. In our opinion, the *voithos* was the most important person in the two-man operation of the commuter bus, maybe even of the whole public transportation system.

There was a legend of a heroic *voithos* who rode on the fender, on the driver's side, when the bus was coming down the mountain and the windshield wipers broke down during a snowstorm. He kept constantly clearing the windshield with his hand until they arrived at the city hospital, just in time for the lady passenger to give birth.

Those who had higher ambitions would say they would be an *elengtis* (an inspector) for the bus line. An inspector was the one who checked the tickets to make sure every passenger had paid the right fare. Our idol was Makis, a local man who had graduated from the Commercial School of Tsagarada a few years earlier. He always wore the company uniform: a blue vest, dark-blue pants, and an officer-style cap, which he wore slightly askew. We thought he looked like the army generals from war photographs we were seeing in magazines.

At the time, I was probably the only one in my group of friends who didn't aspire to become either a helper or an inspector for the bus company. When someone asked me what I was going to be when I grew up, my quick answer was, "I am going to be a captain, like my grandfather. He had his own two-masted *kaiki* and sailed with her all the way to Alexandria in Egypt and to Napoli in Italy." My announcement of career choice always met with Father's approval and encouragement, and sometimes even a coin for candy and a pat on the head.

Then, when I was near the end of what would be the ninth grade at an American school, the Greek government, in an attempt to address the shortage of merchant marine officers, modified the admissions requirements for maritime academies. It was amended so that students with only three years of high school rather than the full six could be accepted, provided they could pass the rigorous entrance examinations.

When I heard about it, I rushed to tell Father I wanted to take that entrance exam at one of the captain-teaching schools. To my dismay, his approval of following in his father's footsteps seemed to have suddenly disappeared. He reasoned that all the schools were too far away from home. At the time, the nearest of the kind was in Aspropyrgos, about a half-hour drive west of Athens, which, in his opinion, was too close to the big city. I wouldn't even be sixteen years old in my first year at that school, he said, too young to be among much older classmates, far away from home, alone in a place full of unscrupulous people and unimaginable temptations. When I pointed out that Lord Nelson, Columbus, and even our own, the great shipowner and patriot, Miaoulis, had signed onto a ship much younger than I, he gave me his usual answer: "Those were different times; the youngsters were more mature, and the grown-ups more honest back then."

He finally agreed to let me take the entrance examinations to the Maritime Academy of Lamia. Perhaps he did it because Lamia was closer to home—approximately halfway between Athens and Volos—

or because it was primarily an agricultural town, and farmers, according to Father, were honest, God-fearing people as opposed to crooks and deviants of the big-city-dwellers. Or maybe he was thinking the entrance exams would prove to be too much for someone with only three years of education in the humble Commercial High School of the village of Tsagarada.

I took the entrance exams in early September, and the results came in the mail two weeks later. I PASSED!!! Father and Mother both told me "Bravo" and "Congratulations," but, from both, the words seemed to be lukewarm. Writing about it now, after having watched my own children go away to college, I can understand why. But, no matter how they had said it then, I don't think it would have matched the jubilation I felt.

CHAPTER TWO

My First Year at the Maritime Academy

The Maritime Academy of Lamia was a school for marine engineers only; not as glamorous as a captain's life, but they visited the same places, and if it meant going to sea and traveling the world, I was willing to compromise.

Now, with my old-age wisdom, I've concluded that I was better suited to be an engineer than a captain. Presently, the occupation I'm best suited for is slow walks in the park—when not too hot or too cold—and midday naps, but back then, I had the curiosity to search and find out why things were the way they were, what made them work, and what would happen if something changed. I had no concern then—and I still don't—how others perceived me, had no worries about face-saving, and no qualms about going from plan A to plan B, if I saw that plan A didn't work. Both good traits for engineers and entrepreneurs, but not necessarily for captains of ships, where image perception is of importance.

It was lucky to rent a room at a new house just one block from the school, with a second-year student at the academy renting the room next to mine.

My years at the academy were maturing years. It was my first time away from the village where harmful temptations were very few, and where my day's activities were prescribed and strictly supervised by my parents and by my teachers, who were on a first-name basis with them. In Lamia, I was free to do practically whatever I wanted.

Almost every one of my classmates seemed to be old hands at city life. I, on the other hand, had visited the city of Volos only a few times, so, in the beginning, I went about my life by watching and mimicking others. In my ignorance, I could have been mimicking the wrong guys. It would be easy to get into trouble. Some believable lies would suffice for my landlady to send a favorable report back to my parents, and if I got a bad grade on a test, the teacher wasn't going to meet my mother after church to tell her about it. But once again, Providence, it seemed, was looking after me.

For certain, it was a case of providential intervention that Philipas Gianacopoulos was renting the other room at the house where I was staying. By being one class ahead of me, he became an excellent tutor and a good advisor about life in a strange city. He was a rational and careful individual who always thought everything through and spoke as if every word was to be carved in stone.

He came from a small mountain village, not far from Lamia, which was also the birthplace of the couple who owned the house. While I rented there, a few times on special occasions, like the name day of our landlord, Mister Sourlis, or a local holiday, they would have a party, invite a few other people from the same area, and ask Philipas and me to join them. Soon after the main meal was over and a few glasses of wine drained, everyone would be belting out local folk songs. I had never been to any activities of that kind before, and I felt awkward, like an outsider whom everyone stares at, as if I had just arrived from another planet. It was a feeling that would come to me a few more times later in life when I found myself among people doing things I was not familiar with. Philipas, on the other hand, seemed to be making friends and having conversations with everyone. With my teenager's knowledge of life, I had placed him in the category of those methodical men who put in their time at their job to the maximum required limit for their retirement, then return home to collect their pension, run for the village council, and live the rest of their lives as respectable members of the community. Perhaps that's why I was so shocked when I met him again a few years later doing something I thought he would never do. But I'm getting ahead of myself.

Although Philipas acted as my tutor and advisor, he was one class ahead of me and spent most of his time with his own close friends and classmates. I became close friends with a group of four guys in my own class, all of whom happened to be levelheaded, had strong work ethics and basic morals, and were familiar with city life.

The first one I met, maybe because he was closest to my five-and-a-half-foot height or because I liked his easy-going, self-assured manner, was Giannis Antoniou. He was friends and roommates with the three other guys, whose names were Thanassis Gramatikos, Giorgos Leondiou, and Dimitrios (Mitsos in slang) Kontogiorgos, who, because of his large size, was nicknamed Mitsaras (big Mitsos). All three of them were of enviable height.

They, and Philipas Gianacopoulos, introduced me to life outside the village, almost in the same way a grown-up takes a child by the hand to the county fair for the first time. As I look back now, I think of myself extremely fortunate to have met them.

Thanassis Gramatikos was a meticulous recordkeeper whose school notebooks and papers were always in order. He was also a stamp collector, a hobby he kept up to his last days. He came from a small mountain village called Kastelia but had attended high school in Athens, where his older sister lived.

Giorgos Leondiou seemed to be the most mature of the group. He came from a small town on the prairie of Thessaly. He was a good athlete and never did anything that could be harmful to his health.

Giannis and I on the third year at the academy

"You'll end up shriveling like a sickly bean in a few years," he would admonish us when he saw one of us lighting up a cigarette. He had the looks of a movie star, and the girls flocked to him, but he did not capitalize on it. He was going to marry his high school sweetheart as soon as he started earning an income, he told us.

I saw my first movie under the guidance of Giannis Antoniou. It was a Western starring Jeff Chandler shown in an open-air theater on the terrace of a building near Park Square. A few minutes into the movie, Jeff Chandler got trapped in a ravine with Indians all around shooting at him. I fidgeted, gasped, and called out to Giannis, "He's going to get killed; he better take cover."

"Don't be stupid," Giannis answered unperturbed. "He's the lead man; they never die the first ten minutes." He was right. A moment later, Jeff Chandler, firing a pistol with his left hand and a rifle with his right, shot every Indian from both sides of the canyon and galloped away.

Giannis Antoniou, I, and Thanassis Grammatikos on a First of May outing in 1958

I lost my virginity in Lamia. My first intimate contact with a woman happened in the red-light district near The People's Square one evening, when some boisterous classmates dared me. The only thrill I remember was that I ended up bleeding when we finished, and the girl put some disinfectant on the cut that burned. Again, I was lucky: among all the girls available there, I happened to pick one who was understanding and considerate, and who took the time to help prevent me from being traumatized by the experience. On my last trip through Lamia a few years ago, I noticed that the shabby red-light district had become a touristy spot full of souvenir shops and quaint eateries. The building where my first carnal experience took place was now a real estate office, painted in bright pastel colors.

Also, in Lamia was the first time I worked for someone other than my parents, and I got paid for my labor at the end of the day. Once during our first year, during a brief break of classes, too brief to travel back home, I, Giannis Antoniou, and the other three of our group took a job at a brick-making factory. (It seemed the allowance from home never lasted beyond the second week of the month.) The work consisted of picking up the boards loaded with freshly shaped bricks as they came out of the forming machine and transporting them on our shoulders to a drying area about a hundred feet away. By the end of the day, both of my shoulders felt sore, and every muscle in my body ached. Mitsaras and Giorgos Leondiou, who were the physical fitness instructor's favorites—Mitsaras, the shot putter champion of the school, and Giorgos, the gymnastics star—were showing off to the rest of us.

Mercifully, we were laid off a few days later, when the batch of bricks the factory had an order for was finished. Some months after that, we tried the allowance-supplementing approach again. We hoed the cotton plants in a field near Lamia. This time, it was much easier; I had lots of experience doing similar work in our garden in the village, and it was my turn to show off.

Later that same year, during gymnastics training, while doing some flipping, Giorgos Leondiou overshot the mat and landed on his head, which caused him to break his spine near the neck. We visited him in the hospital every day. I remember standing next to his bed with the other three of the group, telling him he'd be up and running in a few days. He seemed to believe it, and we did all we could to look like we did, too. He died two months later.

*

Unlike the teachers I had during the elementary and high school years, very few of the professors' names at the Maritime Academy have survived in my memory. Most of them had the air of the *elite-school professor* and didn't encourage much informal association, but the one professor I still remember vividly is Mr. Pagouropoulos. I close my eyes, and I can see him: a broad-shouldered man, standing by the blackboard, his head almost reaching to the top of it.

He taught thermodynamics, boiler design, and ship's steam engines. He didn't do it for the money; he owned a big construction company that, at the time, was handling major government contracts. I think he did it because the academy's director was a relative of his. They both came from Amalota, a remote mountain village outside Lamia, and he probably wanted the graduates of the school that his nephew ran to be just as good as, if not better than, the graduates of the uppity academies in Athens and Piraeus. He had degrees from prestigious universities in Germany and England, where, apparently, he had focused all his attention on absorbing only the engineering knowledge because he still spoke and behaved as if he were in his village among fellow Amalotans.

Maybe it was because of his size, his position, or his knowledge, or maybe because he deserved it. Still, everybody, even the fierce and strict academy director, had a lot of respect and esteem for him, despite his lack of finesse. One time, Mr. Pagouropoulos ordered coffee during the class break from the coffeehouse next door. The man was late in bringing it, and our class had already started when the coffeehouse proprietor himself timidly knocked on our classroom door, offering the tray with the coffee cup and the glass of water on it.

Mr. Pagouropoulos told him to take it away. "You should have brought it when you were supposed to," he said. The director, through his half-open office door, caught a glimpse of the man on his way out and offered to bring the tray himself. As soon as he opened the door, the professor sent him away, too.

"We got work to do now, Kostaki," he said, calling him with the diminutive of his first name, something only relatives and intimate friends usually do. The whole class saw our fierce director deflate, hunch his shoulders, and turn around to carry the tray back to his office.

Getting through Professor Pagouropoulos' classes unscathed was always a challenge. For the first half of each class, he would ask a few of us, one at a time, to go to the blackboard to solve a problem based on his previous lecture. If you stumbled while doing it, he would say, "My boy, if there is something you don't understand during the lecture, ask me. That's why I'm here. No shame in asking, that's how you learn." But then, if you dared to raise your hand and say you weren't clear on a certain something, he would say, "My boy, these are basic, simple things. If you don't understand them, then… what're you doing here? You should go to Amalota and hunt foxes." Fox hunting in Amalota must've been considered a low-intelligence task because he would always suggest it to those he accused of ineptitude.

To Professor Pagouropoulos, things that seemed to us gargantuan, insurmountable problems were as easy as breathing. "Where did you read that?" he would ask if he didn't like the answer to one of his questions.

"In *Douzinas*," we usually answered. At the time, that Greek textbook was considered the bible of every aspiring engineer.

"Pff," he would scoff. "That's ancient. Sit down and learn some German and French or English; they have modern textbooks for today's engineers."

Back then, tourists had not yet discovered our country, and foreign words were seldom heard outside the movie houses or the jukebox parlors. In our English classes, we struggled to get a handle on the basic conversational sentences, let alone the tongue-twisting, incomprehensible engineering terms. Professor Pagouropoulos spoke all three of these languages as if he had grown up in those places instead of the fox-infested village of Amalota.

*

Eastward, about thirty kilometers away from Lamia, was the seaside village of Agia Marina. On the weekends, when the weather was hot, and when we could afford the bus fare, we would go there and swim. Unlike the beaches in my area where the bottom drops quickly and you can be over your head just a few meters from the shore, in Agia Marina, you could walk thirty meters away and still be only waist-deep in the water. I remember the first time we were at the beach with Theodoros Siomopoulos, a classmate who came from a small town in the plains of Thessaly. He had been swimming in the freshwater ponds and lakes near his town, but never in the sea. On his first plunge, when water got in his mouth, he tried to swallow it and started gagging. "It's salty, it's salty," he kept repeating in awe. The poor fellow got teased about it for a long time.

*

During my senior year at the academy, I felt it was time to assert my independence. Philipas Gianacopoulos had graduated and was already sailing on a freighter, and I wanted to do something different. I moved out of the Sourlis' house into an apartment near *Platia Laou* (People's Square). I shared a room with Panagiotis Diamandeas, another classmate three years older, whose father was friends with my father. Diamandeas liked listening to rock-and-roll music and partying more than studying, but we managed to graduate before we got into any serious trouble. At his suggestion, we enrolled in a guitar class taught by the director of the city band. The director was a meticulous and energetic man, and the band under his direction had won many awards for its performance in Greece and overseas. The instructor spent the first week of class teaching us how to read the pentagram and place the notes on the correct lines. I did very well in that part and was looking forward to giving Carlos Montoya and Andrés Segovia some stiff competition. During the second week, the instructor played the notes on the piano and asked us to name them. It was a disaster. Despite my best effort, I did terribly at that part. At the end of the session, the instructor said it appeared I had the ear of an artillery gunner, and it would be hopeless for me to continue. That ended my aspirations of becoming a great guitar player.

Diamandeas also stopped going to the music class because the man was not teaching the kind of music he liked to play, he said.

*

When I reached my senior year, some of our classmates and I, who felt brave enough, corresponded in English with people from other countries around the world. It was done partly as a hobby and partly as an exercise for the English class and, probably, because cell phones hadn't been invented yet. We usually exchanged a one-page letter and some photographs every two or three months with people close to our age who lived mostly in English-speaking countries, like the United States, Australia, and England. I was corresponding with a girl who lived on Olive Street in the city of Elizabeth in New Jersey. She wrote that she was in her last year of high school and planning to go to college to become a teacher. We exchanged photographs, and I wrote to her that she was very beautiful, and she replied that I was very handsome. In the beginning, it would take me over a week to compose a one-page letter. First, I wrote a sentence in Greek, then substituted the words with the English ones I picked out from the dictionary. She must have gotten lots of laughs reading things like, *I play end guardian in the foot sphere team of our school.* In her reply, she asked if I meant I was a goalie on our soccer team. She would correct all my grammar errors, and I would write back that I did it on purpose, so she could practice her *teachering.*

During the spring break of that year, I happened to be in Volos one day, and while walking along the waterfront with Diamandeas and Bouloukos, another classmate, we saw an American Navy ship docked in the quay. "Let's see if we can get some American cigarettes," said Diamandeas, and we went closer. Urged by the other two but also seizing the opportunity to show off my knowledge of the language, I approached the shortest of the two sailors standing guard at the gangway, a man about my size, thin, with glasses, and I said, "Hallo, welcome to Volos," in my much-rehearsed English.

He smiled, and I think he said, "Thank you," and "It is a beautiful city." I asked him if he had any cigarettes, and he said he didn't smoke. Diamandeas asked the other sailor for a cigarette, but he too shook his head.

"Let's go," said Diamandeas. "We'll come back when they change guards." It was the first time I spoke with a bona fide foreign person, and an American at that, and I wanted to linger a bit longer.

"What state of the United States do you come from?" I asked the sailor with the glasses.

"I come from the state of New Jersey," he said, and I thought he grinned as he said it.

"I have one pen pal in the state of New Jersey," I said, after running the sentence in my head.

"Is that so? What city?" he asked. I guessed they had been instructed to be nice to the natives, and I thought his interest might be fake, but when I said, "The city name is Elizabeth," he took a step closer.

"Really, Elizabeth you said? I'm from Elizabeth. What's the address?" I had received a letter the day before, and I had been carrying it in my back pocket for showing off purposes.

"He's from the same town she's from," I called to Diamandeas, waving the envelope toward him.

"*Malaka*," (jerk), said Diamandeas. "He'll steal your girl." I showed the envelope to the sailor, and I thought his face had a startled look when he glanced at it.

He called to the man standing guard on the other side of the gangway. "Hey, look at this." He pointed to the return address on the envelope. "She's my next-door neighbor. This guy here is pen pals with my next-door neighbor, can you believe it?" he asked another sailor walking by on deck to take his place and motioned me to wait. He ran on board and, a few minutes later, came back with an official-looking document with his picture on it. "Look here," he said, pointing at a line that said, "address." It was the same street name, and his number was two digits higher than the girl's. "Next door," he said, moving his palms back and forth against each other. “Next door, small world, huh?”

With some effort, I made him understand that I could put a note of his in my next letter if he wanted. He went on the ship and came back with a writing pad and scribbled a few lines on a page while repeating over and over, “Can you believe it, isn’t that something?”

About two years later, the *Andros Sea*, the tanker I was on at the time, did go to the city of Elizabeth, in the state of New Jersey, in the United States of America, but that’s a story for later.

*

One month before the end of my last year at the academy, an ocean-going freighter laid up in Stylida, a small coastal town twenty kilometers from Lamia. The academy director arranged for the senior class to have a tour of the ship, and one morning, we boarded a chartered bus and went to Stylida. For most of us, it was the high point of the year.

All the ship’s crew had been sent home except one oiler who stood as a watchman. While giving us a tour of the ship, he told us that in maritime parlance, this type of ship is called “Liberty.”

“They mass-produced them in America to fight the Second World War,” he said.

At the start of the trip, the director told us that for main propulsion the ship had a triple-expansion, reciprocating steam engine, the kind we had spent a whole semester studying, and I was looking forward to seeing it. When we descended into the engine room, I was awed; everything was much bigger than I had imagined when looking at the textbook pictures: the pistons were huge, the connecting rods the size of tree trunks, and the crankshaft was almost the size of my father’s truck. The cylinder heads of the main engine had been removed, and the tour guide, who saw us staring inside, pointed out that the low-pressure cylinder was over two-and-a-half meters in diameter. Until then, the biggest engine I had seen was the one of the road grader when they were enlarging the road in my village.

All of us were awed except Bouloukos. One of his relatives had gotten him a job the previous summer on a coastal passenger ship which had diesel engines for main propulsion, and he acted as if the engine room of this ship was way too ancient.

Near the end of the tour, someone asked for a drink of water, and the guide passed around a full pitcher and paper cups to everybody. "You're drinking water from Lebanon," he said. "Our last port was Beirut. We unloaded nine thousand tons of bagged flour from Vancouver."

Although I was thirsty, I drank mine in small swallows, as if tasting a new kind of wine.

I was the last one to leave the ship and the last one to board the bus. I kept looking back, wondering what the ship *I* was going to sign on would be like.

As it turned out, the first and the last ships of my merchant marine sailing career were just like that one; "Liberty" class, but that too is a story for later.

*

In Greece, when a man reached a certain age, he was supposed to report to a certain place stated in the local newspaper for the physical examination and subsequent enlistment in the military. It was the law, and there was no way around it. At the time, the normal length of service was two years, and most young men usually planned their career moves around fulfilling their military obligation.

So, when the names of the boys my age from the area I came from appeared in the newspaper of Volos, I also showed up for my physical, thinking somebody screwed up and left my name out of the announcement. It turned out that none of the government people sitting at the long tables at the reporting place could find my name listed anywhere in their thick books. As far as they knew, I didn't exist.

After doing some searching, I found out that during the Civil War, the partisans had set fire to many county courthouses in the area, which destroyed many important records, my birth certificate among them.

There was a law at the time stating that when someone was a graduate of a Maritime Academy, he could apply for deferral from enlistment until he had accumulated enough sea service to qualify for the third engineer's license. Then that individual could enlist in the Navy as an officer. I was planning to take advantage of that law by proving I did exist, so I could get a seaman's book and go to sea, but that turned out to be a bureaucratic odyssey. Finally, after many back-and-forth trips between Volos and Athens, I was able to get the *phylladio* (the seaman's book), receive the deferral-of-military-service certificate, and I was allowed to leave the country.

CHAPTER THREE

In July of 1961, one week after graduating from the academy, I was on the bus heading to Piraeus to look for a ship. I was ready to explore the world and see first-hand the exotic places I had read about in the novels of Kavadias and Joseph Conrad. I didn't know any shipowners, or any shipping company personnel managers, or even a shipping company janitor, but still, for some reason, I felt confident I would do all right. The talk going around at the time about a maritime recession and of ships lying idle for lack of cargo didn't seem to have dampened my spirits. I headed to Piraeus, where most of the shipping companies headquartered, to start knocking on doors, asking for a job.

Again, I think it was Providence that got involved in getting my first ship, the ship that in later years gave me the right to talk with the old-timers about the good-old-days of seafaring. It was definitely a case of extra-good luck or *favorable coincidence*, as one of my enlightened professors would call it, or, as my mother would say, the angel God had assigned to look after me was wiser than I was.

Bouloukos, a classmate at the academy who had sailed the previous summer, advised me to stay at the Omonia Hotel in Athens. "It's cheaper and safer," he said. "The metro station is almost under the hotel, and in twenty minutes you're in Piraeus, in the middle of every shipping office in the country."

I arrived in Athens late on the evening of August fifth, with a beat-up suitcase and a brown bag with what was left of Mother's almond cookies. The clerk at the Omonia Hotel, a short, middle-aged man with an unshaved face and shifty eyes, said they were full. "They're coming down from the hills in droves," he said, laughing. "I only have one bed left in a double room, but I'm keeping that one for myself. I lie down for a shuteye when we're filled up like this."

Head down, I started to leave and was almost at the door when he called after me: "I'll let you have it at half price if you don't mind me lying down for a few minutes after midnight. You won't tell the boss about it, will you?"

I thought he sounded like a smart-aleck city-sleeker, the kind I tried to avoid, but it was almost midnight, I was tired, and the suitcase felt heavy. I didn't know of another hotel around, nor how long the search for a ship would last, or how far the money I had in my pocket would carry me. In the village, I slept with my brother in the same bed. He was five years younger. He snored and kicked and flung his arms around, hitting me in the face, just when my dream was getting to the good part.

I took the half-price bed. "You don't kick in your sleep, do you?"

"I'll stay at the far end, you won't even know I'm there," he said and escorted me to the room. The man on the other bed was sound asleep.

I got into the bed quietly and soon I was sound asleep. I dreamt I had left home on a long voyage and camped outdoors for the night, sleeping under an olive tree, on a bed made of fresh-cut fern, using my sack of clothes for a pillow. Then, as I tried to stretch, I felt a snake slithering up my legs. I screamed and jumped up. The night clerk rolled out of my bed, zipped up, and dashed out of the room.

My scream woke up the man in the other bed. He turned on his light, sat up, and asked what had happened. I told him. "Damn pervert," he chortled. "Now I'll never go back to sleep." He lit a cigarette and headed for the bathroom. When he returned, he adjusted his pillow and sat in bed, upright, smoking. "All my years, I hadn't heard about that kind of deviants till the last couple of years. It's like an epidemic," he said.

Looking at him from where I was, I guessed him to be about thirty years old. He had black curly hair, a triangular mustache, and the strong, tanned hands of a man who spends a lot of time working outdoors.

"Last year, a pervert like that got a job as a baker in my village," he went on. "The second day on the job, he tried to mess with the butcher's son, but the boy got away and ran to his father. I was away at the time, but they told me it was quite a sight to see: the baker, holding on to his breeches and running out of the village, the women throwing rocks at him as he went by, and the butcher two steps behind, waving his cleaver, and swearing he was going to castrate him."

I asked him if he knew the baker's name, but he didn't. "Same thing happened in my village," I said as I lay back in bed. "The man tried to mess with the priest's daughter. The barber next door heard the girl scream and ran into the bakery. They chased him out of the village, too. I wonder if it was the same guy."

"It's too many of them, they're all over." He took a puff on his cigarette and cursed the damn pervert once more.

I reached the nightstand, took out a cookie, and then held the bag toward him: "Have a cookie," I said. He took one and chewed it slowly.

"This is good," he said. He took another. "Where did you get them?"

"My mother made them."

"They're good. Where do you come from?"

"I'm from Tsagarada," I said. He just stared at me, and I figured he didn't know where that was. "It's a village on Mount Pelion, fifty-three kilometers east of Volos," I clarified. He told me his name and asked for mine. I told him, and I asked where *he* was from. He told me he was from Trikala.

"We're almost neighbors," I said. "Trikala is not more than two hours from Volos."

"What brings you down here?" I told him, and he seemed surprised. "Do you know anybody in the business?" he asked. "Nobody's hiring right now, ships are laid up all over."

"I know," I said. "Last month, the school took us to a freighter that was laid up in Stylida because the owners couldn't get any work for her. I'm planning to go to Piraeus and knock on doors, hoping somebody will hire me. I got pretty good grades at the academy."

"Come with me in the morning, I'll introduce you to our hiring man of Handris Shipping; he's a good man, he might have some ideas," he said.

"Are you a seaman?" I sat up straight on the bed.

"I've been sailing as a deckhand with them for three years now. I'm supposed to be on vacation, but they called me back yesterday; somebody jumped ship in New Orleans, and they're shorthanded on one of their ships that's coming to Lisbon."

"I'll be glad to come," I said. "You don't think he will mind?"

"No, he's an easy-going fellow. Besides, that's his job. Good night." He put out his cigarette, turned out his light, and lay down facing the wall.

I said, "Good night," and turned off my light. Then, with eyes wide open, I stared toward the ceiling, thinking: *Lisbon, New Orleans, what do they look like? Will the hiring man tomorrow be of any help? Handris Shipping is an old company; they have permanent people, like this deckhand from Trikala, they call when they need them. But maybe he knows of a hiring man of another company that might need an engine-room cadet.* I promised I would light candles and put extra coins in the collection plate of the church of Saints Taxiarhes and the church of every other saint in the village if they were to intervene to God and arrange it for me to get a job on a ship.

*

In the morning, he and I were the first to arrive at Handris' office. After a short wait in the reception room, we were ushered into a wood-paneled office. My roommate from the hotel introduced me to a balding, elderly man sitting behind a large desk. I handed him the envelope containing the government papers, my seaman's book, and the academy diploma. The man told my roommate to see Captain Stareas in the next office about his ship, then adjusted his glasses and started examining the contents of my envelope. He went over each line of every piece of paper in there slowly, as if he had just learned how to read. While he was doing that, I studied the ship models of freighters and tankers in glass cases on the shelves of the office walls and, once again, I repeated the night's promises to Saints Taxiarhes and all the other Saints of my village.

Finally, he set the papers aside and looked up. "It's a lucky day for both of us," he said, smiling. "The engine cadet on one of our freighters had to be taken to the hospital in Palermo yesterday with a ruptured appendix." He held up a brown notebook on his desk. "I have a book full of names, but none of these men can be here on time; the *Maritihi* is going through the Canal tomorrow afternoon. If you pass the physical, you can leave in the morning and get on board the ship in Port Said."

He called out a name, and when a man about my age appeared at the door, he told him to drive me to the doctor. "Stay with him till he's finished, then bring him back here."

On the way, the office man asked me where I was from. I told him I was from Tsagarada and explained where it was. "Oh, you're a mountain man," he said, sounding as if I had told him I was from Mars. After that, I noticed his face would form a grin when I seemed awed every time we passed a tall building or a fancy storefront. Then, when we arrived at the doctor's, he told me to be careful crossing the parking lot and did the same as we were approaching the revolving door of the building.

There were many people waiting to see the doctor, and it was almost noon when he examined me. When he finished, the man from the Handris' company got the envelope with the doctor's report, and we headed back to the office. After one block, he stopped by a souvlaki stand. "The doctor gave you a good report; it means you're going on the ship," he said. "Will you treat me to a souvlaki to celebrate? It's way past noon, we haven't had anything to eat, and it only costs one drachma, anyway."

"You can have two," I said, and I ordered one for myself also.

At the office, the personnel man was occupied with some people visiting from the headquarters in London, and I didn't get to see him till almost the end of the day. When he finally talked to me, he welcomed me to Handris Shipping and said their man would take me to the airport early the next day. Then asked his secretary to make copies of my papers, called the man who had driven me to the doctor, and gave him some instructions while I waited outside his office. Soon after, the man drove me back to the hotel Omonia. He walked with me to the registration and told the lady that his company would be paying for my room that night.

Before leaving, he told me that he'd be taking me to the airport in the morning. "At six o'clock, be right here," he said, patting the back of the couch in the lobby. I thought he was treating me as if I were stupid, and for an instant, I felt like punching him. But then I remembered how in the village, my friends and I used to think that big-city tourists were slow-witted critters and used to laugh at the way they tiptoed on the cobblestone paths as if crossing a minefield. Instead, I also patted the back of the couch and said: "I'll be sitting right here." (Many years later, in America, I was introduced to the saying: "What goes around, comes around.")

On the way to my room, I noticed the man from Trikala sitting in the lobby drinking coffee. I hadn't seen him since he introduced me to the personnel man at the shipping company, so I walked over and asked him how his day had gone. He said his ship had been delayed getting into port, and he was staying another night. I told him what happened and thanked him for the introduction. "You must have an angel looking after you," he said.

I offered to treat him to dinner, which he gladly accepted, and we went to the restaurant on the hotel rooftop. We got a nice table, ordered wine, and took in the view. The last rays of the setting sun had painted the tops of the tallest buildings around a soft reddish color, and there was a gentle breeze blowing from the sea. We were two men in perfect harmony with the world. On the street below, masses of people were coming and going, like the steady flow of a human river. "I bet you they're the same people walking back and forth," he said. "Can't see how much humanity can fit in one town."

It had struck me as odd that a man who had sailed on big ships and had been to so many foreign countries would say something like that. "Athens is a big city," I said, "the biggest in the country. Haven't you been to cities just as big on your sailings?"

"Yes, but I never looked at them from this high up. I guess things seem different that way," he said.

That night, before going to bed, I wedged the chair under the doorknob to keep it from opening from the outside.

*

Of the trip to the airport the next morning and of the flight to Cairo, I remember almost nothing. I remember that it was with Olympic Airlines and that it was my first time on an airplane. I guess the person who said, "I should have written my memoirs while I still remembered them," was someone like me. At the Cairo airport, we were met by a man from the shipping agency, who transported those joining ships to Port Said in a white minibus. The only thing that stuck in my mind was how long and straight the road we drove on was; it seemed to go on and on, the far end disappearing in the desert haze.

There were a few other crew members who were going to join mine, and possibly other ships, but either because of shyness or fear of appearing ignorant about travel, I didn't interact with them. In Port Said, I don't remember any of the harbor activity or of the ride with the motor launch to the anchorage where my ship, the *SS Maritihi,* was waiting her turn to transit the Suez Canal. The entry in my seaman's book states it was July twenty-fourth, 1961.

(Many years later, when I took up writing as a form of self-torture, I wrote the novel *Searching for Ithaka*. In it, Kostas, the main character, is signing on board the *SS Marika* in Port Said. He gives a vivid description of his arrival in Cairo, boarding his ship, and transiting the Suez Canal. All of that was based on experiences from later trips as a crew member on the *Maritihi* and other ships, and as a consultant for shipping companies after I stayed ashore in the United States. Some trips were as late as the seventies, with the last one being when my wife, Brenda, and I took a cruise of the Eastern Mediterranean in 2010.)

On the *Maritihi,* I signed on as an engine-room cadet at the pay rate of twenty-one English pounds per month. In my signing-in paper, in parentheses, it said: *performing oiler's duty*. That innocent-looking parenthetic notation meant I would be standing a regular oiler's watch, berthed in the crew's quarters, and eating in the crew's mess hall, rather than the officers' dining room. It was a legal maneuver the shipowners had created to keep the number of crew members to an extreme minimum.

In those days, under normal practices, a ship's engine crew consisted of the chief engineer, the first assistant engineer (who worked from eight to five), a second engineer (doing the four-to-eight watch), two third engineers, three firemen, three oilers, and an engine-room day worker called the *donkey man*. Also, an engine room cadet would be working alongside the chief and first engineers. The cadets of the engine and bridge departments were considered officers. They worked from eight to five and berthed and ate at the officers' side of the ship.

Shortly before I went to sea, the shipowners, claiming a shortage of available manpower, a severe slowdown of marine charters, and an urgent need to cut operating costs, had gotten permission from the government to consolidate some of the ship's chores. And so, onboard the *Maritihi*, the first assistant engineer was performing second assistant's duties, and I, the engine cadet, was serving as one of the oilers and getting an oiler's pay. (Which, actually, was a bit more than I would earn as a cadet.)

I started on the eight-to-twelve watch. My cabinmate was Nikolas, the fireman of the same watch. He was plump, around forty, had a shaved head, and one gold tooth in the front. He had the bottom bunk, and I got the top one.

Although I remember nothing of the first and second days on board the ship, other than Nickolas' instructions to keep everything locked tight while transiting the Canal, I'm sure, as I watched the shores of Egypt fade behind the ship's stern, none of the great explorers felt more anxious and more eager to see the world.

Nickolas told me the ship was loaded with bagged flour from Amsterdam for Surabaya. "It's in Indonesia," he hastened to clarify.

At Kartalion Elementary School in Tsagarada, there was a laminated map covering half the north wall of our classroom. I remember looking up Indonesia during the geography lesson. It was near the bottom of the map, on the right-hand side, just above Australia.

For my first trip, I was going to the other end of the world! I was starting out with a "Bang."

The third engineer of my watch was Mr. Pandelis Patsas, *Mastro Pandelis*, as everyone called him. (Just as the bridge officers have the prefix *Captain* in front of their names, the engineers on Greek ships have *Mastro* in front of theirs, presumably derived from the word *mastoras*, an adaptation of the English word *master*.)

Looking back at it now, I think it was more than a stroke of good luck. It was, like the man from Trikala said, a Divine intervention, a guardian angel who arranged for me to get the job on the *Maritihi* and to be on the same watch with Mastro Pandelis.

Mastro Pandelis was in his late sixties at the time, short and round and counting the days until his retirement. He came from Milies, a big village on Mount Pelion, about thirty kilometers from Tsagarada, and, since we were practically neighbors, I guess he felt a comradeship and paternal obligation to look after me. He guided me through the minefield of shipboard life that awaits a newcomer, defended me against the old-timers' dislike of *book engineers,* and shielded me from the wrath of the chief engineer, a grumpy old man from Hios.

He gave me a slow and thorough tour of the engine room, explaining the purpose and the quirks of each piece of machinery as he went. "The slide-valve on this feed pump sticks sometimes; when you're starting it, crack the steam half a turn and give it a light tap with the hammer." Then farther over on the main engine: "When you're lubricating the cross pins, do it on the downstroke so the oil won't hit you in the face." He said the Americans had installed automatic lubricators for that job, but when the Greeks got the ships, they took them out because they thought they were using too much oil.

He told me the Americans called this type of ship *Liberty Class.* They were built during World War II to carry supplies to troops in Europe and Asia. "In their day, they were the most modern things afloat," he said. "They were building them all over the country. This one was built in Hoboken, New Jersey. The shipyards were launching one of these a day, and that's what broke the Germans' back; you don't mess with the Americans."

Part of my duties as an oiler on the *Maritihi* was to make rounds at certain intervals during my watch, usually every hour, and lubricate the main engine slides, the crank pins, and cross pins, the shaft bearings, the steering gear bearings, and everything else that needed lubricating. Lubricating a reciprocating triple-expansion steam engine of a Liberty ship while it was running was a challenge. I stood on the grating, halfway up the engine block, and when the cross-pin was at a certain point, I would squirt one shot of oil from my oil can. It took three squirts per side of each cross-pin every hour. Then I would do the same on the slide-valve guides. It was a tricky operation and, until I mastered the technique, my right hand was permanently black and sore from colliding with the rotating crosshead. Twice, the oil can was knocked out of my hand and landed in the engine sump. The chief engineer threatened to dock my pay for it, but, thanks to the resourcefulness of Mastro Pandelis, we managed to retrieve it without stopping the engine.

Also, once every hour, I had to make rounds and write on a slate the temperatures and pressures of the components essential for the engine function: water, steam, fuel, etc. I would bring the numbers to Mastro Pandelis, who was stationed permanently under the ventilator next to the control board, and he would record them in the engine log.

The transit of the Suez Canal and the Red Sea went smoothly. I made my rounds when I was supposed to, I made sure every bearing and every slide got its deserving share of lubricating oil, and I brought the coffee to Mastro Pandelis on time, without spilling it.

On the trips to lubricate the steering gear, I would always pause on deck and stare at the gray silhouettes of the distant shores we were passing. During the first few days, I kept to myself. I was shy and hesitant to join conversations with the rest of the crew; they all seemed much more experienced with life on board a ship. One evening, Kotsios, a burly, easy-going deckhand on the same watch, while making his rounds on deck, saw me staring at the outline of an island on our port side, and I guess he thought it was homesickness.

He stopped next to me and teasingly asked, "What was her name, Thodori? Better forget her, she's already found someone else." He laughed and showered me with spittle. "That's Socotra you're staring at, there are no women there; nobody lives there, but don't you worry my friend, when we get to Surabaya, I'll take you to a place where a sweet young thing will make you forget everything you left back home; you'll be like the guys in *Odysseas'* boat when they ate the lotus fruit."

When we entered the Indian Ocean, the good ship *Maritihi*, although fully loaded, started pitching and rolling, and I was sure we would sink at any moment. I was seasick the whole week that followed. Everybody said this was the roughest they'd ever seen the Indian Ocean, but that didn't make me feel any better. Every roll of the ship would send my stomach darting from my head to my toes and back up again. I kept throwing up even when there was nothing in me to throw up. Mastro Pandelis was constantly feeding me crackers and dry toast to absorb the liquids in my stomach, and urging me to keep on moving, but all I wanted was to lie down and die. I remember spending most of my time on the watch in one corner of the engine room, lying on top of a stack of evaporator coils that I was supposed to be cleaning.

The rest of the crew kept eating and smoking and walking about, although on peculiar angles, as if they were strolling in the park. I would never be like them, I thought. It was enough to catch a whiff of smoke or see someone chewing on a sandwich to get me running to the side and belch. I was constantly thirsty. I was having visions of lying by the side of a crystal-clear stream, gulping ice-cold water. Again and again, I cursed my idea to become a seaman and promised myself that if I got out of this alive, I would become a shepherd and live on top of a mountain, far away, where I couldn't see, hear, or smell the sea.

Then the ship entered the Malaga Straits, and the vicious sea was transformed into a mercury pond with not even a ripple on its surface. My stomach settled back to its original position, and I forgot all about becoming a shepherd and living on a mountaintop. Life was good again. I was glad to be alive, and, like the rest of the crew, I looked forward to our arrival in Surabaya. It was the first foreign port I would be seeing as a bona fide merchant seaman, and I was eager to start my collection of enviable experiences: to feel the breeze of "magical, exotic tropical nights," as a popular Greek song of the time said, and see the rich tropical landscapes. And, equally important, the women, the "sweet young things" who Kotsios said would make me forget about ever going back home.

We docked in Surabaya on August twenty-eight, during my first watch. Using the pretense of going to check the steering gear, I went on deck as many times as I could and leaned on the bulwarks to take a glimpse of the harbor and the city beyond. Closer by, the line handlers were dragging the ropes of our ship toward the mooring bitts while shouting at each other in a strange language. Men in suits holding briefcases and uniformed policemen stood on the dock waiting for the deckhands to lower the gangway. Trucks sped up and down the pier, beeping their horns and belching smoke. Outside the harbor gate, taxis and rickshaws picked up and dropped off passengers. The air had the smoky, sour smell of an industrial area.

I drew five pounds from the captain, which gave me a pocket full of rupiahs, and was ready to start my exploration as soon as the chief mate issued the passes. It turned out that neither my cabinmate nor Mastro Pandelis wanted to go ashore the first day. "It'll take them about a month to unload us," they said. "We'll have plenty of time to see the place." Kotsios, the deckhand who had said he would show me all kinds of thrills in Surabaya, got sick and had to stay in bed. I ended up going later that afternoon with three men from the deck department who said they had been there before.

My first night out in an *exotic tropical land* was a disappointment. The place where the taxi driver took us was a trashy shanty town with a bad drainage system. There was a full moon, which shed a soft light over the palm trees and the blooming bougainvillea, but the gentle tropical breeze brought the smell of open sewer and decaying garbage. The women were not the hazelnut-exotic beauties dressed in long, body-fitting gowns with slits way up their thighs and flowers pinned in their hair that I had seen in magazine photographs. They were ordinary black, flat-nosed girls wearing convenient-for-the-job, wrap-around skirts. And, as I found out during my first intimate contact with a foreign woman, her perspiration had a sour smell. There was no lotus fruit effect, for sure.

Two days later, I went ashore after my morning watch with Nikolas, my cabinmate. Following his example, I stuffed my pockets with a dozen cigarette packs. After we passed the harbor security gate, Nikolas negotiated a one-hour sightseeing tour with a rickshaw driver for six packs of Marlboros. We settled in the back seat, and while the driver pedaled away, we took in the sights. "We're like two English lords inspecting the colonies," I said, and we both laughed.

In some of the streets we were passing, there were European-style houses and almost all of them in need of maintenance: their plaster was cracked and peeling, and the paint faded. "Those are the remnants from the Dutch colonial days," said Nikolas. "The country was part of what they called Batavia. They got their independence not too long ago. It'll be interesting to see what they'll look like a few years from now."

At a crowded market, we traded the rest of our cigarettes for a bundle of rupiahs. I bought a few postcards that showed the port of Surabaya from above, a silk scarf for my mother, a Japanese lighter for my father, and something for my brother and sister, although I don't remember what they were.

We sat at a sidewalk table of a small café, ordered three orange sodas, and asked our rickshaw driver to join us. He was thankful for his soda, but he said he preferred to drink sitting on his rig. The drinks, although barely a couple of degrees lower than the stifling midday heat, felt refreshing, and we took small gulps while watching the masses of the natives going about their daily chores. Most of the men were dressed in wide-legged pants and vests, almost as long as coats, and wore a fez. The women wore long, colorful dresses that looked like bedsheets wrapped around their bodies.

"In some ports," said Nikolas, "I take the public bus. I ride it all the way to the end of the route and back. That way, I get to see the locals going about their regular lives. It gives me a better feel of what life is like in that country."

I thought his idea made sense, and since then, when I am in a foreign city and I have the time, I do the same thing.

During the voyage, I wrote a letter to my parents. I told them that on the airplane, I sat by the window and could see Athens and Cairo from high above, and that they were both huge cities. My parents had never been on an airplane. "The flight was smooth, and it took only two-and-a-half hours to get from Athens to Cairo, in Egypt," I wrote. "During the flight, they served us drinks, and the plane had toilets in the back, and we got to use them while we were up in the air." I also told them about the long, straight road on the drive from the airport to Port Said.

Someone reading this might have difficulty understanding why I would think a straight stretch of road worth writing home about. If so, that would be because they don't know that in Greece during my youth, straight stretches of paved roads longer than a mile were very few, and only in storied places. My father, who had traveled them with his truck, talked about them with the same awe as if he had seen the Taj Mahal. It took the battered public transportation bus four hours to journey that gravel, potholed road from my village to Volos, where the longest straight section was less than fifty meters. There were lots of people from our area who had migrated to Egypt, and when they came back for a visit in the commuter bus, it took them a while to get over the car sickness. While waiting for their innards to get back to their original place, they would brag how smooth and straight the roads were in Egypt. (Most of the locals, when they traveled to Volos, made sure to sit by the window for the fresh air and always carried a lemon or an orange to smell along the way as prevention against car sickness.)

About the transiting of the Suez Canal, I said that the only way I could describe it was that it looked like a huge ditch where the ships lined up, one behind the other, like sheep returning from the pasture.

I also described how big a ship the *Maritihi* was. "In our cargo holds," I wrote, "we are loaded with ten thousand tons of flour from

Holland. It is bagged in sacks; thousands and thousands of them, to unload in Surabaya, in Indonesia." (My father often transported sacks of flour for the general stores of the villages on our mountain. In my mind, I could see him comparing the ship's capacity to his Dodge truck.)

I wrote about my duties and about having Mastro Pandelis Patsas, a man from the village of Milies, as the engineer on my watch. (When I returned home some months later, my brother told me that Father had gone to Milies asking if anybody knew a man by the name of Pandelis Patsas, and what kind of person he was.)

Before mailing the letter home, I added another page describing the city of Surabaya in the tropical country of Indonesia. I made no mention of the turbulent Indian Ocean and of the torturing sea sickness.

*

It turned out that my cabinmate was right: it took the stevedores three and a half weeks to unload all those thousands and thousands of sacks from our cargo holds. That gave me time to make three more sightseeing trips with Nikolas, sampling the native food at a couple of restaurants and talking to the English-speaking rickshaw drivers about the history of the place. By then I had come to understand that the "fun palaces" that are the traditional first stop of a mariner are not the best places to get an idea of what a country is like.

We left Surabaya on a rainy day on September eighteen, heading for Marmagoa. The chief mate said it was a small town in the bottom of India, in a Portuguese colony called Goa. From there we were to load bauxite for Japan.

It seemed the same storm that almost convinced me to become a shepherd was waiting for me again in the Indian Ocean. The huge waves made our empty ship roll from side to side even more than before, but this time I could eat, smoke, and walk around in peculiar angles like the rest of the crew. I was cured!

With the ship being empty and high out of the water, Mastro Pandelis and I would take turns during the watch operating the *butterfly*—a primitive mechanism the Liberty class ships were equipped with for protecting the engine from over-speeding. It involved standing by the high pressure column of the main engine and listening to the sound of the pistons going up and down. When the sound became lighter, it meant the propeller was coming out of the water and the engine was picking up speed. We'd hasten to pull on the long lever that closed the butterfly valve which reduced the steam supply to the engine, slowing it down, and preventing serious damage. A couple of seconds later, we'd push on the lever to open the butterfly again allowing the engine to resume its normal speed. If the valve stayed closed too long, the steam pressure in the boilers would build up and cause the safety valves to pop open. For a fireman to "pop his safeties" was a black mark and, when it happened, it usually brought the chief engineer running down to the boiler room to give the fireman a royal ass-chewing. The popping of the safeties might have prevented the boilers from exploding, but it did so by allowing the extra steam that accumulated while the butterfly was closed to go to the atmosphere, which meant the distilled water and the precious fuel used to make that extra steam was wasted. To the super frugal Hiotian captain and the chief engineer, that was an unpardonable sin.

Because my body was of the *economic size* variety, short and light, I struggled more than others getting the butterfly back to the open position. I'd put all my weight on the handle and kick my feet in the air, but the damn thing still wouldn't move, which made the fireman on watch, shout at me to hurry it up while he scrambled to shut off the burners. Newer ships of that period had sensors and regulators installed in the critical points and all these tasks were interconnected and done automatically without skinny engine cadets and overweight firemen having to strain themselves.

During the voyage, when the weather was calm and Mastro Pandelis wasn't occupied with his engineering chores, he would spend the watch standing under the ventilator. It was at a spot from where both the engine and the boiler gauges could be seen and that allowed Nikolas, the fireman to come over and join him. The two would spend most of the four-hour watch swapping food-related stories from ports around the world. Mastro Pandelis had sent money to his daughter in Volos to open a bakery with her husband, and most of the time, he would be telling Nikolas about the pastries, the breads, and the baked dishes he was going to teach them how to make based on what he had tasted during his sailing years.

Usually, their conversations went something like this: "A steward I sailed with married a Cuban and opened a restaurant in Havana," Mastro Pandelis would start. "His wife was a chef, and she did all the cooking. Her specialty was a meat dish she called *Ropa Vieha*. It has beef, onions, peppers, green olives, and all kinds of other stuff in it. It's all cooked in a pot with some kind of Cuban tomato sauce, and she used to serve it over yellow rice. It tasted out of this world. I'm getting hungry just thinking about it. I always asked for seconds when I ordered that one. Last time I was there I convinced her to give me the recipe."

Then Nikolas, who also knew how to appreciate good eating, would reply. "There is a Greek restaurant in Buenos Aires, right by the water, not too far from the docks, that serves a steak three fingers thick and two palms wide; it fills the whole plate. And it's so tender you can cut it with your fork. I used to get it with a salad, Greek-style potatoes and a bottle of his homemade wine. I think the owner was giving me extra attention because he was looking for a husband from the old country for his daughter." He would pause to wipe his neck and face with the sweat rag and then continue: "We used to load bones from there and take them to England. There is no worse cargo than bones; worms crawling all over the ship."

"It couldn't be any worse than the guano we hauled from Chile," Mastro Pandelis would counter. "The stink could choke you; I couldn't eat anything the whole trip. But I made up for it when we got to England. I had fish'n chips and shepherd's pie every day. In Southampton, there is a pub owned by an old Greek who worked in the kitchen on the P and O ships. His pies were the best; he used only young lamb for them. Then when he took it out of the oven, he would crumble some feta cheese and sprinkle it on top, it was to kill for."

"The best fish'n chips I ate were in Boston, in a little shack next to the main gate of the port, run by a black man. He'd never tell me what was in the batter he dipped the fish in before frying it, but I couldn't get enough of it. He used to serve it with fried potatoes he called French fries. He showed me how to eat them with a kind of tomato sauce he called *cat soup.* I asked him if it had parts of the cat in it and he laughed his head off. I liked the taste and now I put that cat soup on everything, even my eggs in the morning."

"The American black people are good at grilling meats, especially ribs," Mastro Pandelis would reply. They call it *bar, mbee-ee, que*. And they have sauces with all kinds of flavors. There is a place in New Orleans that …"

It was like this on every shift, the whole four hours of it. By the time the watch was over they had covered the ports of all four continents.

*

Two weeks after leaving Surabaya we dropped anchor in Marmagoa Bay, within sight of the loading dock. We were among twenty other ships, with flags from Norway, Sweden, Greece, England, Panama, and Liberia, all patiently waiting our turn to take on cargo.

The loading was done by an ancient, slow-moving steam-crane with a leaky bucket. It took almost a half hour to dump a shovelful of ore in the ship's cargo hold. "Must be a Portuguese operation," commented Mastro Pandelis. "An American company would have installed electric cranes and conveyors and have us loaded before we finished tying up."

During those years, American prestige was at its peak and Mastro Pandelis, who had spent some time in that country, was a great admirer of anything American. That was the time before *modernization.* Before people of all countries started buying clothes made in the same places, the places with cheap labor. And before everyone everywhere could watch the same shows on their television sets. The word globalization did not exist, even in the dictionaries. The satellites and the internet that made the exchange of information to the far reaches of the globe, faster than you can deliver a letter across the street, were known to very few of the common people. Container shipping, which made commerce among the countries of the world efficient and inexpensive, had not been invented yet. Each country had its own styles and its own ways of making things and that was reflected in their people. Back then, when you saw two men walking down the street, you could tell which one was the Brit and who was the Frenchman, by the clothes they wore and by the way they groomed themselves. (I thought about the loss of that ability many years later, while waiting for my wife to come out of the British Museum in London. I was watching the hordes of tourists from different countries entering the museum and, unless I saw the flag or the sign held high by the tour guide ahead of the group, I couldn't tell if the people following that guide were Spaniards, Greeks, or Romanians.)

During the two weeks we were at anchor in Marmagoa waiting for our turn at the loading dock, those who didn't want to take the boat launch to go ashore, the old-timers mostly, spent their afternoons sitting on the hatch covers critiquing the ships around us. "I bet you that one," an old-timer would start, "the one with the funnel round like a fifty-five-gallon drum, is an English job. They haven't changed their design since they invented steam."

Then another would add: "The one on our stern, with the sleek lines, is definitely Italian."

"And that Liberian bulker, on our starboard bow," someone else would cut in, "the one that looks like a slipper with all her superstructure aft and the black smokestack tall and slender like a stove pipe, I bet you she's built in Japan and belongs to the National Bulk Carriers."

On the SS Maritihi, 1961, in Moruray, Japan

"I think you might be right," another would agree. "I knew a man who had been a third mate in one of the ore-carriers of that company. He told me that the owner was an American named Daniel Ludwig. He said when he ordered his ships, he told the shipyard 'If it doesn't carry cargo, do away with it.' He owns freighters and tankers, all of them built in Japan and all of them are like that one: plain, with no frills. I hear their pay is the best in the business and the crew on his ships can eat as much as their stomach can hold."

During that era, food on Greek merchant ships was the major topic of conversation; there never seemed to be enough of it. The most common cause for fights among the crew was when someone ate one of the snacks left by the steward for the men on the night watches. It seemed there was competition between the captains of each shipping company as to which one of them would go the farthest below that budgeted feeding allowance. When we met a crewmember from another ship the first thing following the greeting was, "How's the food in your ship?"

After all these years, I still have a vivid memory of the exchange between the captain of the *Maritihi* and Nikolas, my cabinmate, during dinnertime one day. Nikolas had been working on cleaning the starboard boiler and had just sat down to dinner. The captain, an old, stubby man with a limp, was coming down from the bridge on his way to the officer's mess, and, as he passed by our dining room, heard Nikolas fussing at the mess boy about the small piece of meat on his plate.

He paused in front of the door and addressed Nikolas:" "Hey Nikola," he said in his thick accent, typical of a thoroughbred Hioti, *"inda ehis kai fonazis?"* (What's making you protest?)

"This meat portion," answered Nikolas. "It's not enough to feed a sparrow, let alone a man who's been working hard all day."

"Do you know how many grams of meat the union contract calls for?" the captain asked.

Nikolas had read the contract and had the answer ready. "This piece here isn't even half of it," he said.

But the captain also had his answer ready: "Darn it Nikola, that's how much it is. Out for the bone, out for the fat, that's what you got left. I never thought I would have to explain that to one of our own."

Later, when we went in the cabin, Nikolas vented his frustration by kicking his canvas bag stored under his bed. I think, more than losing the argument, it was the captain calling him *one of my own* that upset him so much. Although he was born in Hios, Nikolas had lived most of his adult life in Piraeus and he'd only admit any association to that island if it involved some kind of praise. "This son-of-a-whore of a captain will starve us to death," he said when he finished punishing the bag. "Last trip he fed us shark meat."

"I didn't think the ship chandlers sell shark meat," I said.

"No, we caught the shark ourselves. We were two days out of Zamboanga, loaded with copra from the Philippines for Amsterdam, when a gasket on the main steam pipe busted. We drifted for almost three hours while the engineers were putting in a new one. It was early in the morning, on a dead-calm day and the bosun took it upon himself to do some fishing while he stood by at the anchor windlass. He caught a small shark, about a yard long, and that damn, saint-robber up there," he gestured toward the bridge, "had one of the lifeboats lowered and brought it onboard. We had shark meat for the next two days. Until then I only had heard stories of starving castaways eating that kind of fish."

"How did it taste?" I asked.

"It was not bad, better than some of that freeze-burned ox meat the cook had been serving us, but the captain acted like it was choice steak from Argentina. Every time he sat down to eat, he would broadcast, loud enough to be heard all the way down to the bilges, what a good fisherman the bosun was and how lucky we were to have a meal with this delicious fresh fish. Damn miser, he sailed on the Livanos ships for a while and, I guess he was trying to copy the people-fooling tricks old man Livanos used."

"What did Livanos do?"

We had laid down in our bunks and Nikolas was leafing through an old magazine. "One time one of the Livanos' freighters," he said, a bit louder this time, to penetrate the mattress of the upper bunk, "made a stop in Bermuda for bunkers and old man Livanos flew over from New York for a visit. They did not expect him, and the steward got all shook up when he said he would join them for lunch. I was told that the cook on that ship was so bad the crew had been threatening to throw him overboard. 'We're having *pastichio* today, Mr. Livanos,' said the trembling steward, 'perhaps you would like the cook to prepare something lighter for you, instead?' 'My boy,' said the old man, 'of course I'll have the *pastichio*. That's the main reason I came here.' The steward brought him a plate, and he ate every bit of it, while raving, loud enough as if everyone around him was stone deaf, that this was the best *pastichio* he ever ate. Then, sounding as if he was speaking through a bullhorn, asked for seconds, and after that he asked the steward if there was any of it left. 'I would like to take some home, so my wife can see what good *pastichio* tastes like,' he said."

Nikolas lit a cigarette and after exhaling he went on. "I would bet the old goat threw the bag in the trash as soon as he was out of sight and probably puked his guts out, but the cook and the steward felt invincible after that. Complaining to them about the food you got the same result as when hitting a granite wall with a feather ball."

In my later years on merchant ships, I discovered that there were many legends—some true, some made up—circulating in the maritime world about ship owners and captains from Hios. It was known that shipowners preferred to recruit men from their place of origin because they perceived them to be more loyal. It was not unusual to hear a Hiotian captain tell a compatriot colleague: "In my crew, I have twenty of ours and ten foreigners." The *foreigners* being those from parts outside the boundaries of Hios.

On the other hand, the foreigners would say that the shipowners from Hios preferred to recruit their own because they were slow-witted and easy to please. A story circulated among the foreigners at the time about a Hiotian sailor who went to the captain and asked for a raise. "My boy," said the captain, "do you know how much you're making now?" "One English pound a month," answered the sailor. "There! You see? In a thousand months, you'll have a thousand pounds. You can be a shipowner, but I'll still be a captain."

On the *Maritihi*, there were three foreigners in the engine crew: Mastro Pandelis, one fireman from the island of Kalymnos, and me. On the deck department there were only two foreigners, two deckhands. One was from Piraeus, studying for the third mate's license, and one was from Athens, who, although in his early thirties, everyone called Barba Elias (Uncle Elias) on account he was always taking a philosophical view about everything in life, like an old man. (In the Greek slang, the word *barba* means uncle and is frequently used to address elderly men as a sign of respect.)

Elias had sailed as a second mate on a small, coastal freighter around the Mediterranean Sea, but wanted to see more of the world and had signed on the *Maritihi* a few months before I came on board. He spoke some French and English and although he could have gotten the post of the third mate with a higher salary, he opted to sign on as an ordinary seaman. When I asked him why, he told me he didn't want to put up with all the ass-kissing that comes with the higher-paid job.

One evening, two days after departing Surabaya, a group of us were sitting at the poop deck swapping adventure stories from different ports while watching the seagulls dive at the propeller wash. The bosun said he thought the taxis were too expensive in the last port and he had opted to walk. "I like to hold on to what I'm making; I work too hard for it," he said. "Now, if I was rich, I would go around in a long limousine."

"I would do the same," added another, "and I'll have a pretty woman by my side." Then someone else said if he was rich, he would have three women, one on either side and one to serve him drinks. "How about you?" someone asked Barba Elias who sat farther away, smoking. "What would you do if you were rich?"

"I would get a limousine too, but I'd let it go in front and I'll walk behind it," he answered.

I was about to ask him what he meant by that but right then somebody shouted to look at a seagull that nabbed a big fish, and after that, the conversation drifted to fishing and to other things.

*

In Marmagoa, the land of fakirs and snake charmers, I had planned to do a lot of sightseeing until the captain announced that everyone should stay close to the docks. He said there was fighting at the outskirts of the town between the occupying Portuguese army and the Indian liberation movement and foreigners were not allowed beyond the town limits. So, in the evenings, all of us gathered at the ramshackle bars along the waterfront: the multinational crews from the ships anchored in the bay, the Portuguese soldiers guarding the colony, and the local pimps and their merchandise. We drank room-temperature beer and sang the popular songs of the time in a cacophony of languages. (The Italian song *Marina, Marina*, that was popular then comes to mind.) We danced, swapped stories, and traded whores, a real United Nations affair.

I got to know a Portuguese soldier about my age and size who played the guitar. He showed me a picture of his fiancée: a pretty girl on a beach, sitting next to a large heart drawn on the sand.

One of those evenings, during shoptalk in mutilated English sentences with my counterpart of a Russian bulker, I mentioned that I might leave my ship in the next port and try to get on one with more modern propulsion engines. The Russian engine cadet seemed surprised.

"Can you do that? You said you've been on board only a few months."

"We sign on for a year," I said. "But I can leave any time I want. Only, if I leave before my year is up, I'll have to pay for the ticket home."

The Russian seemed to ponder this new information for a while. "I can't do that," he said. "I've signed up for three years and if I leave early, I have problem, big problem." That short answer during that brief conversation between two men of similar occupation and equal social standing, did more to decisively answer the question of why I wouldn't like to live in Russia, than the fancy rhetoric of all the politicians and propaganda peddlers from both sides.

Near the end of our last afternoon in Marmagoa, a commotion on the street in front of the Happy Mariner Café hurled us off our bamboo chairs and got us lined up at the edge of the thatched patio to see the parade. What we saw was Barba Elias, his black cap tilted way back, his shirt slung over his shoulder, walking leisurely between two rickshaws while a girl in each one was blowing kisses to him. When we started clapping, they also blew kisses in our direction.

"What is that crazy fool doing?" the bosun from our ship mumbled a few feet away.

"There goes a true bohemian," said a man from a British ship behind me.

I turned around and asked him: "What is bohemian?"

"A man who lives unconventionally," he answered. Then seeing I didn't understand he added, "A man who lives the way he likes to live and doesn't give a hoot what other people think." Seeing my blank stare he quickly added, "doesn't care what the others think about him."

"That's our Elias, exactly," I said.

Everybody talked about Barba Elias' parade the next day.

"I was trying to make a point to the bosun," he told me later. "He's sucking up to the chief mate and shorted me four hours of overtime, but I don't think he got the message."

CHAPTER FOUR

From Marmagoa we headed for Muroran, an industrial town in one of Japan's northern islands. We were loaded to the top of the Plimsol marks, so our deck was low in the water. As the ship rolled with the swell, we could almost touch the waves. Quite often, when I went on deck during my night trips to check on the steering gear, I would pick up the flying fish that had the misfortune to land on deck. After the watch, Nikolas and I fried them for a midnight snack. It was a pleasant substitute for the cheese-and-mortadella sandwiches the steward usually left for the night watch.

Muroran had lots of steel mills and tall smokestacks belching black smoke. There was a lot of pollution in the air and people, the elderly mostly, walked about wearing masks. It was the first time I saw people doing that outside a hospital, and I thought it was odd. Now, as I write this, my home state of Alabama is in the middle of the worldwide coronavirus pandemic, and the United States government advises everybody to wear masks. I never thought that there would come a time when that piece of cloth would become an essential part of one's wardrobe.

On the second week in Muroran, I met a girl at a nightclub with whom I ended up spending the rest of the time the ship was in port. She spoke very little English, and we communicated mostly with improvised sign language. We must have thought that was very funny because we both giggled and laughed a lot. She was a sweet young girl and, I think, she worked as a secretary for a shipping company. She had a small, tastefully decorated, one-room apartment with a mattress on the floor.

During the time the ship was there, a photographer came on board and took photographs of anyone who wanted to have something to remember the occasion by. She was a middle-aged lady with a sweet smile and a motherly disposition, and she got a lot of customers that day. I remember she took quite a few pictures of me on deck and in the engine room but the only one that has survived through the years is the one of me and two of the firemen standing in the engine room. The thinnest of the three is me. The largest is Nikolas, my cabinmate.

It was a pleasant stay and when we left, I hoped we would make another trip to that town. I still remember how to say in Japanese: *Thank you very much. I love you. Wait a minute my friend*, and some other phrases, not suitable for mixed company.

*

From Muroran we sailed empty across the North Pacific to Vancouver, to load bagged flour for Colombo, in Ceylon. We ran into a storm south of the Aleutian Islands and Mastro Pandelis and I had to take turns standing by the engine column operating the butterfly again. In most ships now, everything in the engine room is automated. The main engine and all the auxiliary machinery are equipped with overspeed controls and automatic lubricators, and those on watch spend their time sitting in cushioned chairs in front of control panels in air-conditioned rooms. *Lucky people!*

This time the butterfly valve was harder to move than the previous times. Mastro Pandelis said it was because of the new packing we put in Muroran. Nikolas, the fireman, kept darting from one boiler to the other, constantly opening and shutting the fuel supply to the burners, trying to keep the steam pressure high enough to keep the engine turning at normal speed, but below the limit that would make the safety valve open.

On the second day of the storm, halfway through the watch, I was relieving the engineer on the butterfly, when the damn thing stuck closed, and despite Nikolas' quick actions, the safety valve of the starboard boiler popped, filling the engine room with a long-lasting thundering sound. Almost instantly the chief engineer came sliding down the ladder. He got to the operating platform, just in time to see me struggling to move the lever and open the valve. I had straddled the valve lever and was kicking my feet in the air as if I was riding a wild bronco in an American rodeo. He shoved me aside and gave the lever the strong jolt that did the trick.

As soon as the safety valve closed and the thundering stopped, and his voice could be heard, he started chewing out Mastro Pandelis, who had just returned from checking the temperature of the tail-shaft bearing. Then, when he finally ran out of insults and curse words, he turned around and went up the stairs toward his cabin. He paused on the top step to deliver one last volley. "This is the job for the engineer of the watch," he shouted, "not for the oiler or the fireman. It won't hurt you to get some exercise."

Mastro Pandelis was silent during the entire chastising storm. Although he kept nodding, his face had the look of a man whose thoughts were engaged with other, more important things. I think I know what it was: He was counting down to his retirement. "When it feels like you're about to get angry about something," he had said to me during one of our earlier conversations under the ventilator, "think of the reason you're *doing* that particular *something*, it'll keep you from getting into useless arguments." I was sure, while the chief engineer was bombarding him with insults, Mastro Pandelis was thinking of the hot loaves of bread, the shepherd's pies, legs of lamb, and pastries coming out of the oven of his daughter's bakery in Volos.

The next day, the captain changed course, and the waves were hitting from the port side. Although the ship rolled more this time, the propeller did not come out of the water as much and we took a break from wrestling with the butterfly. While taking a break from my chores, I mentioned the chief engineer's outburst about the popping of the safety valve the previous day.

"In my time," Mastro Pandelis said, "in the days I was a fireman on coal-fired boilers, it was exactly the opposite. Then the firemen bragged if they ever managed to *pop the safeties*. It meant they were strong and were shoveling the coal in the furnace fast enough to keep up with what the engine needed and then some." He let out a sigh, repositioned himself under the ventilator, and went on. "Those days the firemen were the ones running the ship. When I first went to sea I started out as a coal trimmer, that was the man who transported the coal in a wheelbarrow from the storage to the hopper next to the boilers.

Then three months later I got to be a fireman. It so happened I was one among the group who hung the herring in the boiler room, you might have heard about it."

"I think I did," I said. "Didn't it have something to do with forming the seamen's unions?"

My question seemed to have fanned some dormant embers in the old man. He moved to a different spot under the ventilator, ran the sweat-cloth over his face, and took a deep breath. "We were the ones who brought all the betterment in this business," he said finally. His voice had become strong, confident, and full of authority. "Before us, when you signed on a ship, you had to bring your own cup and plate and even your own bedding. At mealtime, you took your plate up to the galley window and the cook would dump a ladle-full of slop in it. You ate it and then washed your own plate. Didn't have messboys bringing the food to you and doing the dishes and changing the bedsheets every two weeks."

"What did the herring have to do with it?"

Mastro Pandelis ran the sweat cloth over his face and around his neck one more time, then went on: "I had been on that rust bucket for a little over six months. On the trip that we hung the herring we were running empty from Havana to Charleston to load cotton for Manchester. We were behind schedule because the stevedores in Havana had taken too long to unload us, and they were trying to get all the speed they could get out of the old engine to make it to the loading port on time. We were shoveling the coal as fast as we could; the bridge and the chief were thrilled to hear the safeties pop.

"The kitchen had been feeding us smoked herring and a piece of maggot-infested bread for a long while and we finally had had enough. The lead fireman brought his herring down in the boiler room and hung it up in front of the control panel next to the steam-pressure gauge. Then he told us to slow down the shoveling. 'We'll make just enough steam to keep the ship from drifting' he said.

"It didn't take long for the Saint-robber of a captain to come running down to see what happened. 'What are you doing?' he screamed. 'We'll lose the charter if we don't get to Charleston by Monday.'

"'We're weak, every one of us; can't lift these heavy shovels with what we're being fed,' said the lead fireman and pointed to the herring dangling in front of the gauges." Mastro Pandelis took a sip from his water-can then wiped his mouth with the back of his hand. "I'm telling you," he went on, "for the rest of the trip, we ate like lords; as we say back home, *tou pouliou to gala,* (the milk of the bird), they fed us. That was the incident that..."

The horn of the voice tube crackled and Mastro Pandelis dashed to answer it. When he came back, he told me the bridge wanted water on deck, and I went to start the fire pump.

I heard the same story on some of the other ships I sailed on later. It seems that every old-timer claimed to have been on board the tramp steamer on which, a long time ago, a group of firemen staged a slow-down in protest of the working conditions. That slow-down, supposedly, started the maritime strikes which forced the shipowners to make improvements on their ships. The legend of the hung herring had been circulating among the merchant mariners for almost as long as the legends of the mermaids. It would be impossible to find out if Mastro Pandelis was indeed part of the original group that started the movement.

When propulsion engines were installed on ships, it started a rivalry between the bridge and the engine departments. Both claimed their department was the most important in the operation of the ship. Every seasoned engine crewmember had a respectable inventory of stories of screw-ups the topside bunch did, and I'm sure those on the topside had just as many of the down-below bunch. ("Only fools and firemen sit on the ship's bulwarks," a deckhand told me when he saw me sitting there one time while anchored in Marmagoa Bay.)

During the calm periods of our watch, I used to egg on Mastro Pandelis to tell me stories from his sailing years. The one he kept repeating, and which I didn't have the heart to say he had already told me before, was the one that had to do with the rivalry between the two departments.

"It was right after I got to be third on one of Karamenos' colliers," he would start. "The captain on that ship was the most obstinate and the biggest egomaniacal person I've ever known. He tried to blame every one of the ship's problems on the engineers, especially the chief, who was a saint of a man and had double the years of experience than the captain. One day, just hours after we sailed from Malaga, the second was hammering on the anvil, forging a hinge for the carpenter's storeroom door, and the captain heard it all the way up in the officers' saloon. 'Why is the engine knocking today?' He asks me across the table. 'It's because the chief forgot the anvil inside the low-pressure cylinder when we changed the rings in Malaga,' I told him. The radio man told me later that the captain had him send a long telegram to the home office telling what the chief had done and requesting a new chief engineer on the next port. When we got to Alexandria there was a new man waiting at the dock, all right, but it was a captain, not a chief engineer; old man Karamenos, God rest his soul, didn't put up with foolishness like that."

(About thirty years later, I happened to be in Lisbon assisting the port engineer of Hess Oil with the shipyard repairs on one of their supertankers the company had just purchased. During a work-scheduling meeting, the yard superintendent kept calling me Captain. "What you think about this, Captain?" or "Is this OK with you, Captain?" Finally, after the third or fourth time he did that, the vice president for marine operations of Hess Oil, an elderly man from New York, interrupted him. "Don't keep calling the man *Captain*, his mother and father were married." I was told later that the vice president had been a sea-going engineer before being transferred to the main office.) Recently, I read in one of William MacFee's books where one of his characters, a member of the ship's engine crew, referred to the captains as *bridge ornaments*. William MacFee was a British writer and a marine engineer himself; apparently, the feud between departments was a worldwide phenomenon.

*

It took the *SS Maritihi* twenty days to cross the North Pacific. We arrived in Vancouver during the second week of December. Almost every house around the harbor was decorated with multicolored Christmas lights. I remember thinking how strange it was that there weren't any of the usual entertainment places for merchant seamen near the harbor. There were only places which the locals called pubs, where they sat around on benches and drank one beer after another and just talked. No appetizers, no music, and no dancing. I thought that was a barbaric way of entertainment, and I said so. A few of the crewmembers had relatives living in Canada and they said it was a great country; I was just looking at it the wrong way.

In later years, when I traveled to Canada on business and on vacation with my wife, I had the opportunity to explore beyond the harbor districts, and I realized those crewmembers on the *Maritihi* were right: it is a great country.

One of the deckhands, who had been there before and could say a few words in English, took with him a pint bottle of Johnny Walker the first night he went ashore. "That's for bait," he told me. He talked Kotsios, another deckhand, into going with him, and they went to one of the pubs near the harbor. The next day, at breakfast, the one who had the bottle bragged about their conquests of the previous night: "When I let her peek at the bottle in my pocket she said: 'Come, let's go right now.' I said: 'Not so fast sister. I came here with a friend. I'm not leaving him alone.' So, she whispered something to the woman sitting next to her, and then both practically dragged us out of that place and over to an apartment that I think belonged to his woman." He nodded toward Kotsios. "When we got inside the door, she grabbed the bottle with both hands and kept gulping until my woman took it away and started drinking."

"They drained the whole bottle like it was lemonade," said Kotsios. "When we left, both of them were passed out; bet you they don't remember a thing this morning. Putting that bottle in your pocket was a smart move my friend."

"Listen mister super stud," an old timer interrupted him, "taking advantage of some desperate alcoholic is not any different than raping somebody. I wouldn't brag about it if I were you." That seemed to diminish Kotsios' achievement and for the rest of the day he didn't say anything about it.

*

The loading was done using the ship's cargo gear and the way the stevedores handled our winches almost gave the chief engineer a heart attack. They seemed to run them wide open when hoisting the load and when coming up empty-hook. There was constant clanging of the winch pistons and a permanent cloud of fog from the steam escaping from the worn packing glands hovering over the deck.

Every day after our morning shift Mastro Pandelis and I would work four hours overtime on the winches, putting new packing, repairing crank-bearings, and renewing brake bands. The rumor was that we were the last ship the stevedores would load before taking off for the Christmas holidays, and they were working extra posts. The last pallet of flour sacks was lowered in our cargo hold on the afternoon of Tuesday, December nineteenth. We cast off three hours later.

My first Christmas at sea was like any other ordinary day. The radio operator posted on the bulletin board, next to the previous week's soccer results, a message from the company's headquarters in London, wishing all men and their families Happy Holidays. For dinner we had the usual roast beef and potatoes, only this time the meat was freshly purchased in Vancouver instead of the freeze-burned chunks hacksawed from the sides of a retired plow oxen. And, instead of the usual apple or orange for dessert, we had pound cake with cherry preserves on top, also purchased in Vancouver.

On our way to Colombo, we stopped in Honolulu to refuel. Despite the captain's urgings and the chief engineer's valiant efforts to get more speed out of the old engine, we arrived before noon on New Year's Day. I remember hearing the captain's loud voice in the officer's mess hall during breakfast complaining to the chief engineer: "Couldn't you try to get an extra turn on the propeller Mastro

Panagioti? The office is going to burn my ass bringing the ship into an American port during a holiday; they don't like to pay the American overtime."

I had hoped we would tie to a pier and see some of the famous exotic Hawaiian women, but we anchored in the middle of the harbor and the agent and the customs people climbed the pilot's ladder and started their work. The immigration officer refused to get on board like the others, and we had to lower the gangway for him. When he finally managed to get on deck, we noticed the man was blind-drunk.

This time the immigration inspection was done differently. Perhaps it was the frugal captain, trying to shorten the time consumed on expensive American overtime pay, or maybe it was the drunken immigration officer in a hurry to get the job over with and return to his holiday partying. So, instead of getting us to line up at the officer's saloon and checking everyone's papers individually, as was normally done, they told us to gather on top of the Number Four cargo hatch while the inspector stood on the boat deck above and tried to count heads.

All of us stood on the main deck, with the sun directly overhead and sweat running down our faces, looking up to the overweight inspector in Bermuda-style shorts and flowery shirt, on the boat deck. He was swaying slightly right and left—although the ship was perfectly still—counting each one of us with his index finger like sheep in the fold. He kept checking his list and recounting and always coming up one man short. The captain told him the missing man was the fireman who was in the engine room below, because somebody must always be looking after the boilers. The inspector said he wanted to see that man, so another fireman went below to relieve him. When the inspector did the re-count, he came up one man short again, and again the captain tried to explain it was because of the man in the boiler room. "The way it's starting, it'll be a miserable year, I can tell," I heard the captain mumble to himself.

Finally, the fuel barge came alongside and, as we were hooking up the hose, I heard the chief engineer tell the second that we were getting just enough fuel to get us to Singapore. "The penny-pincher on the bridge says Bunker C is almost half the price over there; you say your prayers and hope the weather is with us," he added.

As it turned out, the weather chose *not* to be with us. For most of the trip, the wind was blowing from our bow ushering along huge waves that swallowed the ship and crashed on the bridge bulkhead. The *Maritihi* was rolling and pitching and groaning like a dying old sea monster, making very little headway toward Singapore where the half-priced Bunker C was waiting for us. The chief engineer had me taking the fuel tank readings twice a day and as soon as I brought him the numbers, he would get busy doing complex calculations and scratching his head. I'm sure it was that trip that started his hair graying.

It didn't take long for some old-timers to start reminiscing. Somebody would tell of the time his ship ran out of coal east of the Cape of Good Hope, and they had to burn the hatch covers to make it to Cape Town. Then someone else would try to improve on that tale: "On the tanker *Capetan Mihalis*," he would counter, "when our coal bins dried up outside Valparaiso, we didn't have the luxury of wooden hatch covers, we started burning the furniture. We even ripped the paneling from the captain's cabin."

After departing Honolulu, I asked the bridge cadet, a mouthy runt about my age, how much more was left to our destination. I guess the little prick was feeling witty at the time because he said, "I'll make it simple for you: On the chart, Colombo is this far," he held his two open palms in front of him about one foot apart, "and every day we move only this much," he showed about two inches between his thumb and index finger of his right hand. "Even an engineer can see that we got a long way to go."

We reached Singapore forty-two agonizing days later, and, to the chief engineer's relief, with a few drops of fuel to spare. I happened to be on the deck getting some fresh air before I dove to the stifling heat of the engine room below, when we approached the Malacca Straits. I could see the group of islands from far away, looking like bouquets of flowers floating in the ocean. When the ship was closer, I could make out sparkling-white houses with red roofs scattered among the lush green vegetation of the tiny islands. The sun was about to set, and the few puffy clouds had turned many different shades of orange. It looked like the photographs I had seen in a travel magazine. The sea was calm, and everything was quiet. As the ship glided through the small islands, only the muffled sound of the engine below could be heard reaching the deck, like some distant jungle drum. The deckhand of the watch walked by dragging the sack with the wooden plugs for the scuppers behind him.

"Beautiful, isn't it?" I nodded toward the shore.

"Yeah, Singapore is pretty," he said. "And they want to keep it that way. They'll clip your ass if you spill as much as one drop of oil overboard." He hammered a plug into the deck scupper. "The chief mate wants me to plug every damn hole," he mumbled as he moved on.

Taking on the ship's fuel was the duty of the first engineer with the engine cadet as his assistant. I had to watch the level of the fuel storage tanks by frequently reading a sounding rod of dubious accuracy and inform the first when it was time to stop the filling of that tank. I had to do it early enough to prevent overfilling and spilling the fuel on the deck but not too early which would leave the tank partially empty.

To this day, I'm not sure if it was a faulty-sounding rod, or if I misread the thing, or if I was daydreaming as the first accused me, but suddenly, black, gooey fuel started gushing out of the vent pipe of Number Four Starboard fuel tank. Had there been a raging fire on board or had the ship been sinking, there would have been less panic and commotion than when the deckhand on watch shouted, "Overflow on Number Four Starboard!" Almost instantly, men with shovels, with empty fifty-five-gallon drums, and sacks with sand and sawdust appeared on deck and started scooping up the oil that was spreading on the deck. Somebody opened a valve and somebody closed another, and finally, the vent pipe of Number Four Starboard stopped spewing Bunker C.

It took two full hours to get the deck mopped and cleaned up. Everyone was feverishly spreading sawdust, building little dams with sand to block the flow, and shoveling oil-soaked sawdust into the drums. And all this time the captain stood on the starboard bridge-wing shouting through the bullhorn, instructions, threats, and curses with the island flavor of Hios.

Fortunately, not one drop of the black stuff spilled in the water, which made the chief mate and the rest of the deck crew the heroes of the day. For the first engineer and me, it was a very dark moment. "In this country, they put your ass in jail just for throwing a cigarette butt on the street," he shouted. "What the hell were you doing?" I don't remember what answer I gave him but whatever it was it didn't make any difference. He was convinced I was at fault.

*

We got to Colombo on the afternoon of the twentieth of February. I was showered, shaved, and dressed in my going-ashore clothes even before the pilot's boat came alongside, planning to make up for the dull stay in Vancouver. But soon after the pilot boarded, we were informed, by the smirking bridge cadet, that we would be staying at anchorage for a week because there was no available berth for us. That announcement took all the wind out of our sails. During the long, slow days of traversing the Pacific, most of us younger crew members had been grilling those who had been in Colombo before about the quality of the entertainment places and the availability of trade girls and we talked a lot about all the exciting things we would do when we got there.

The time at anchorage seemed to last twice as long as the entire two months it took to get there. We spent the days lingering on the shoreside of the deck, some trying fishing and others just staring longingly at the port and cursing the cheapskate shipowner for not providing launch service and the stupid Port Authority for not having a dock available.

Finally, the day came when our ship picked up anchor and with the pilot boat leading the way and the tugboats tooting, we were ushered into port. It was Monday, the twenty-sixth day of February 1962. As soon as we were tied up and the quarantine flag came down, a horde of merchants rushed on board and spread their blankets on the tables, on the deck, and wherever they could find a flat surface. Besides the usual peddlers of razors, postcards, and girly magazines, there were merchants selling rubies, sapphires, and other precious stones. There were also tailors who carried a multitude of cloth-samples and promised to finish a suit to our measurements, while the ship was in port.

My cabinmate knew of a man who worked as steward on the passenger ship *Patris* and who was an expert of precious stones. "He buys as many as he can when his ship calls here," he said. "The *Patris* runs between Europe and Australia and stops in Colombo on the way down and back. The man makes an extra salary on every trip."

Mastro Pandelis had been in Colombo before and said the English pound was very strong there. He had gotten some good deals from those merchants.

My first trip ashore was for scouting purposes; I exchanged a few English pounds, which confirmed what Mastro Pandelis had said, and I walked around but didn't venture far from the ship. The next day, my cabinmate, Nikolas, myself, and the assistant cook, hired a taxi and told the driver to take us to a very good restaurant. About thirty minutes later he stopped in front of a European colonial-looking building where a porter in a red jacket with gold ribbons and white gloves opened the door for us. Our driver exchanged a few words with him in their language and left. The porter called a man in a black tuxedo over and he ushered the three of us to a table by a window. From there we could see smooth, rolling green fields and the sea beyond. Two men holding long sticks were hitting small balls about a hundred yards from where we sat.

"He brought us to the country club," said Nikolas. Nikolas, who was the most traveled in our group, had spent a lot of time in Argentina and spoke fluent Spanish. "This is where the rich come to kill time; it's like our *caffenio* back home. Only they play golf instead of backgammon." Then, since neither the assistant cook nor I had ever heard of the game, he went on to explain what golf was.

After studying the menu, all three of us ordered the same thing: grilled fish with rice, steamed vegetables, a green salad, and a bottle of white wine. A tall, black waiter hovered over our table, immediately refilling the water glasses each time we took a sip and emptying the ashtray as soon as we flicked a cigarette.

Our food came on large oval plates covered with silver domes, carried by a procession of waiters in white gloves and long white coats. They landed the plates in front of us, removed the domes, and put three small plates next to them with lemon wedges wrapped in cheesecloth. Then they bowed and left.

The assistant cook stared at the plate in front of him as if he wanted to print it in his mind. If cell phones had been invented, one of us would have taken a picture, I'm sure. In the center of each plate was a large trout-like fish resting on a bed of shredded green cabbage and sprinkled with grated coconut. To one side was rice, molded into the shape of a starfish. At the opposite side, balancing the plate, was asparagus, strips of carrots, and strips of yellow peppers arranged to look like a bouquet.

"It's almost a shame to cut into it," I said.

"Cookie," said Nikolas, "take notes and next Friday you do the fish the same way."

We kept staring at our plates, none of us putting a fork to the food, till one of the waiters standing against the wall, almost at attention, came over and asked if there was something wrong.

"No, nothing wrong," I said, "we wait for the bread to come."

The waiter gave his colleagues a perplexed look. He went away and came back a minute later with the tuxedoed man who had shown us to the table. He asked what was wrong and when I told him, he said normally, bread comes only with sandwiches. After a brief conference, all three of us ordered two ham sandwiches each. When they came, we removed the ham and ate the bread with our fish while the waiters stared at us in bewilderment.

One Sunday, Nikolas and I, and a few others, went on a day-long outing. The agent of the shipping company had arranged for a bus to take any interested crew members of the *Maritihi* on a tour of the countryside near Colombo.

The trip took us through parts of the jungle where I saw banyan trees for the first time. Some of them had roots that reached the ground from higher branches, which took hold and became another tree trunk. The guide said a tree like that could get as big as a city block. The foliage was so dense that sunlight couldn't reach the ground.

At the edge of that part of jungle, a small river ran through an open field. A man on his haunches, perched on a fallen coconut tree watched over six elephants cooling off in the river shallows. For one rupee each, I, and a couple of daring others, rode the elephants through the field and jungle paths for almost an hour. It was like riding on a slow mule, only taller.

After the mini safari, our guide took us to a tea plantation owned by a British company called Four Roses. One of the plantation supervisors, a short, skinny fellow with light-brown skin and blond curly hair, gave us a tour of the place. He spoke English slowly and clearly like someone who has dealt with non-English-speaking people before. He explained how the tea was harvested and dried before shipping it to England to be put in fancy tins and the tiny bags "you chaps dip in your cups," he said. I asked him how long he had been working there. "Since I was tall enough to reach the top of the bush" he answered, but he didn't say how long ago that was.

I watched the women of the harvesting crew lined up next to each other, ten-across, pinch the top leaves from the tea bushes and fill the sacks hanging from their shoulders. It reminded me of the women picking olives in my village. An old woman closest to me looked just like Widow Evanthia, our best olive picker. As I walked by, I smiled at her, and she smiled back, showing gaps between her yellow teeth.

At the end of the tour, we were escorted to a reception room where they offered us freshly made tea and biscuits.

On the way back I pointed to a poster we had seen everywhere and asked the bus driver if it was the picture of a famous movie star from Colombo. He acted surprised and insulted. "No," he said, "she is

Madam Sirimavo Bandaranaike, our prime minister; the first woman in the world to hold such an office." He sounded proud.

We sailed from Colombo on the afternoon of the tenth of April, one week short of two months. Everyone in the crew carried fond memories of the place. Even those who did nothing but sit on park benches and watch the people walk by, said Colombo was a good port. "For a country run by a woman, it's not a bad place," an old-timer mused.

My cabinmate, after lots of thinking, had spent a month's pay and bought a handful of stones. Mastro Pandelis had a summer suit made from a beige-colored, silk-like cloth he called Santacrouta. I didn't buy anything. At twenty pounds a month salary, even with super-favorable exchange rates, there wasn't much left, especially when the ship stayed in port so long.

CHAPTER FIVE

From Colombo we went to Marmagoa again, to load iron ore for Japan. This time, to our surprise, there weren't any ships waiting and we were docked directly under the overaged crane and started loading. We found out shortly afterward that there had been a change of government in the area. The Indian Army had taken over the colony, and we were told the Portuguese soldiers had been taken prisoners. Later that day, a deckhand said he had seen about a dozen of the soldiers working on a road and four Indians with machine guns standing guard. "I saw the guy who was playing the guitar the last time we were here, and I tried to give him some cigarettes, but the guards wouldn't let me get close," he said.

Some of the waterfront taverns that we frequented on the first visit were now closed and the few remaining served only soft drinks at room temperature. A few enterprising young pimps still tried to broker visits to "clean, young girls," but most of us thought it too risky an undertaking. My shore time consisted of leisure walks not too far from the ship, exploring the ruins of an old fort overlooking the harbor built during the glory days of Portugal. I had a lengthy conversation with a turbaned guard at the docks about the new developments and the rights of people to live free and how the liberation of Goa from the Portuguese was like the revolution of the Greeks overthrowing the Turks.

From Marmagoa, we went back through the Malacca Strait to Singapore, for bunkers, on the way to Japan. In the Strait, we ran into thick fog, and we had to slow down. The captain placed every available deckhand on lookout and constantly blew the steam horn, much to the consternation of the chief engineer for wasting our precious distilled boiler water.

We took fuel, without any mishaps this time, and some fresh water and groceries, then headed to Kobe where we unloaded half of the cargo. From there we went to Osaka to unload the remainder of the iron ore. While there, a port engineer from the company's main office came and after the cargo holds were emptied, the ship was moved to a shipyard for structural repairs that the insurance company had requested. (The foundation for the anchor windlass needed reinforcement, some areas of the cargo-hold bulkheads needed welding, and certain pipe sections of the fire line needed renewing.)

For five days, the ship was overrun by shipyard workers in blue boiler suits and white hard hats. Some among the workers had one or two stars painted on the front of their hats; those were the foremen and the supervisors of the group.

In the shipyard, there was a room next to the machine shop, where the workers spent their time during their coffee breaks. There were vending machines for snacks and soft drinks in that room, and I made many visits there to get potato chips and cold orange sodas. Next to the door, hanging from the ceiling, was a canvas punching bag, the kind boxers use for training, and someone had drawn a life-like portrait of a two-star shipyard superintendent on it. Almost every man coming into the breakroom, and before returning to work, would land a few punches on the bag and say a few phrases which, judging from the tone of the man's voice I suspected were of the *unsuitable-for-mixed-company* variety.

A few men from our crew—mostly the married ones—bought in Japan delicate cups and dinner plates with pretty designs on them to take home. A few others bought transistor radios and when we sailed they would walk along the shoreside of the ship, endlessly tuning them, trying to catch a good radio station.

While we were in port, four of us chipped in and bought a guitar. We planned to peck on it in our free time and, hopefully, somebody in the group would learn how to play it. As soon as we left Osaka it started making the rounds of partners. We would peck on it for a week trying to extract some discernable tune out of its chords, then give up and pass it on to the next person. After a while, even non-partners were allowed to give it a try, but despite our best efforts, nobody from the crew could play on it anything that sounded like music. In the end, we concluded the shifty Japanese had sold us a defective instrument and we hung it on a wall in the mess hall.

Our bosun bought a fancy camera and when we left Osaka, he coaxed me to translate the operating manual. After struggling for a week to translate a couple of pages, I gave up.

In Kobe and in Osaka, some from our crew spent a lot of their free time at taverns with Greek names, most of them run by Greek ex-seamen, who had married local women. There seemed to be Greek ships in every port those days. Also in every port, Greek seamen who had stayed ashore. They had managed to get work visas and hang around the ship chandler's and the shipping agents' offices, earning an income as a go-fer. Some of them operated taverns where their jukeboxes played Greek songs full of longing for home and for the woman left behind. It seemed it was the indisputable opinion of the proprietors of those establishments that a seaman's homesickness could only be cured by the purchase in large quantities of overpriced, watered-down drinks of cheap liquor.

After three weeks in Osaka we departed for Iloilo, a small port in one of the Philippine islands. We would load sugar there and proceed to Suez for orders, the mate said. "That means they're not sure where we are going to unload," he clarified. "The guy who's buying the sugar is shopping it around to see who'll give him the best price."

It took us about ten days to get to Iloilo, enough time for the fish-oil the bosun had coated the deck with to dry off. We picked up the pilot about an hour after lunchtime. When we entered the harbor, a fleet of bumboats surrounded the ship hawking everything from green coconuts to dark woodcarvings and razor blades. Most of the crew's attention was directed to two fishing boats with large banners on their sides. One banner read, "The Love Nest Nightclub," and the other, "The Wild Lucy's Tavern." Both boats were loaded with women of various shades and body shapes, all dressed in skimpy outfits. They lay on deck and hung on the rigging, like sailors on a pirate ship, and, with seductive gestures called out to us. "Halo, I'm Lisa. I will be waiting for you at the Love Nest tonight," or "I'm Wild Lucy. Come see me at my tavern tonight."

When the women found out that the ship was Greek, they started throwing at us whatever Greek words they knew, most of which were probably learned from old salts and would make a church-going woman faint. Suddenly, the voice of the captain standing on the bridge-wing, thundered through the bullhorn above all the racket. "You, at the bow! Stop flirting with the sirens and pass the hawser to the line handlers." The poor bosun got a lot of teasing afterward for his well-meaning attempt to be friendly to the natives.

The sugar processing plant seemed to have sprouted out of the dense jungle on the outskirts of the town of Iloilo. The raw sugar started pouring into our holds as soon as the tugs nudged the ship under the loading chute. Then, two days later, they stopped the loading, and they moved our ship to an anchorage, and an American-flagged vessel was put in our place.

It was late in the afternoon, and we sat on the Number Four hatch watching the line handlers tying up the American ship in the spot we had just left. The American was an old-fashioned-looking ship, clean and freshly painted, with the superstructure in the middle, two cargo holds forward and three aft, with masts and cargo booms in between. The smokestack was green and had a white circle with a capital M in the center. At the stern, a large American flag flapped in the breeze.

Mastro Pandelis said the ship that took our place under the loading chute belonged to the Moore-McCormack line. "The Americans have priority here because they built this terminal," he said. "When Castro tried to get tough with Kennedy and cut off the sugar shipments, the Americans built a bunch of brand-new refineries in this country and told Fidel to eat his sugar. You don't mess with the Americans."

"Mastro Pandelis, did you live in Texas when you were in America?" asked a deckhand sitting next to us.

"No, I lived in New York. Why you ask?"

"A deckhand on my last ship had spent a year there before the immigration caught up with him, told me a story, and I was wondering if it was true. He said a Texas man was zooming down the road in his big Cadi-liak when two blacks were crossing the street. He didn't even slow down; he ran right into them. One slammed into the windshield and landed in the front seat and the other got knocked half a block away. When the cops came, they arrested one of the blacks for breaking and entering and the other for running away from the scene of an accident."

"It is called Cadillac you simpleton. And what he told you was a joke. I heard the same joke in New York. It was probably told by the same people who used to say ten Greeks make one negro, until we beat the Italians in the war. There are bigots in every country. Remember the jokes they used to say back home about the refugees from Asia Minor? Most Americans are nice people; they are the kind that like orderliness in their work and in their life. I never had any problems over there from blacks, whites, or any other color. If I didn't have family back home, I would stay there forever."

Between the anchorage and at the loading berth our time in Iloilo was two weeks. Most of the extra pay we got for boiler and cargo-hold cleaning was spent at Wild Lucy's and Sweet Eleni's establishments. Then a few days after we left Iloilo, one by one, the men began to visit the chief mate in his cabin. It turned out that everyone at Wild Lucy's had the clap, the girls at Sweet Eleni's had crabs, and the girls at the Mariner's Love Nest had both. "The chief mate will have to order the penicillin by the gallon when we bunker in Singapore," chuckled my cabinmate.

Before leaving port, a Swedish deckhand by the name of Oscar joined our crew. He was a third mate who had missed his ship, and the agent asked the captain if he could sail with us as far as Suez. The captain said he could but would have to work as a deckhand along with the other day workers to pay for his keep. I don't think Oscar was too fond of the idea, but he grudgingly agreed, and had been following the bosun's orders doing as little work as he could get away with.

Two days out of Iloilo, Oscar and I happened to be working close to each other. He was chipping the rust near the foundation of the anchor windlass, and I was renewing the brake lining of the starboard drum.

I was absorbed at what I was doing, drilling, and fastening the new lining onto the metal band, when suddenly I heard the chief mate shout from the bridge, "Your mother too, shit-pot."

"What did you say?" I yelled back.

"I was talking to the Swede," he answered.

The Swede didn't seem to pay any attention and kept up his odd way of chipping. Before long, the chief mate was next to him, holding him by the collar and telling him if he didn't stop it, he would throw his ass overboard.

"What did he do?" I asked.

"He was tapping curses in Morse Code with his chipping hammer."

"I thought it was something strange in the way he was trying to get the rust off the metal," I said.

I told Nikolas, my cabinmate, about the incident and we both had a good laugh. "When I was on a Livanos ship a couple of years back," he said when he stopped laughing, "we picked up a Spaniard in Buenos Aires. He had missed his ship and, since we were going to Barcelona, the captain agreed to take him if he worked for his fare. That captain was a carbon copy of the one that's up there." He nodded toward the bridge. "When we were one week out of Buenos Aires it was June 29th, the feast day of the Apostles Peter and Paul. Back home it's a big day for the church and a national holiday for Greece, in honor of our King Paul. The Greek ships also observe the holiday and on ours, all those who didn't have to stand watch were given the day off. Shortly after breakfast, Felipe—that was the name of the Spaniard—joined some of the day workers in the crew's lounge in a card game. When the captain on his way to the bridge saw Felipe in his clean clothes, playing cards and drinking coffee stopped and asked him why he wasn't working. Felipe said it was because of the holiday. "This is a holiday for the Greeks, Felipe. It's because of the Greek king; has nothing to do with Spaniards," said the captain. He called the chief mate over and told him to get the bosun to give the lazy Spaniard something to do. Felipe said: 'OK captain,' and went to change his clothes." Nikolas lit a cigarette and while exhaling, he grinned, as if getting ready for the upcoming funny part.

"Then on Monday the following week," he went on, "when the rest of the crew went to work on deck, Felipe sat in the smoking room in his clean clothes, playing solitaire and sipping coffee. The bosun told the chief mate about it, who told the captain, who marched in and asked him why he wasn't working. 'Today is Francisco Franco's birthday,' Felipe said. '*Grande fiesta en Espania.* It is *grande* insult to Generalissimo to be working on His day.'"

"The captain probably knew the sly Spaniard was lying but perhaps didn't think it was worth risking ridicule from the home office by asking for confirmation. We were about a day before crossing Gibraltar and a couple of days later we would arrive in Barcelona where he would be rid of his ass. He told Felipe that he was docking his pay for this *grande fiesta* day, then added a few cuss words and went to the bridge."

*

On our way to Suez, we stopped in Singapore for bunkers. Once again, for some mysterious reason, despite all the pre-bunkering lectures I was given and all the precautions I took, one fuel storage tank did overflow during the refueling operation. But, like before, the quick response of the deck department managed to keep it from spilling overboard.

(Two months later, as I was entering the Maritime Office building in Piraeus, I run into the first assistant engineer of the *Maritihi* exiting the building. He said he was glad to see me and that he wished we could sail together again on another ship. We exchanged a few more pleasantries, talked about the reasons each one of us was at that office and I walked away. After two steps I stopped to tie my shoelaces, and I heard the first talking to the man he was with. "That's the cadet I told you about who kept spilling the oil every time we bunkered," he said. "Good riddance." That brief exchange has stayed with me ever since.

Until then I thought people were saying the same things behind my back that they were saying to my face.)

When we arrived in Suez, a crew of about a dozen Egyptians came on board as line handlers in case the ship had to tie up at a pier during the transit. There were also two electricians who were going to install and operate the mandatory spotlight at the bow for the night transit. That was a powerful spotlight, and when it was turned on, we had to run a separate generator which made the chief engineer grumble for "wasting fuel to shine at the sand dunes."

My cabinmate kept reminding me to keep the portholes shut and the door locked while the shore crew was on board. "They got long poles with hooks on the end, and they can squeeze even a mattress through the porthole," he said. "Even when you're inside, keep the door locked. They try the doors and if they're unlocked and you're inside, awake, they offer to sell you dirty pictures. If you're asleep, you'll wake up on the floor."

Some of the Egyptian workers spread mats on the deck and on the cargo hatches on which they laid out their merchandise. Most of it consisted of postcards showing camels, palm trees and the pyramids and an assortment of souvenirs: bronze and copper decorative plates, alabaster ashtrays and statues of Egyptian kings and queens with headdresses of cobras ready to attack. They sat cross-legged next to their shops trying to coax the crew into buying what they were selling. If the customer seemed to hesitate, the merchant would lift one corner of the mat to reveal a stack of girly magazines. "Want buy pretty girl pictures?" he would suggest. All of them could utter some understandable Greek phrases.

While waiting to join the convoy, one of the two Egyptian electricians came to the crew's lounge and asked if he could get some coffee. He told us his parents were Greek— "One of the few families left after Nasser kicked all the foreigners out," he said. He was a thin, shy-looking fellow, and spoke Greek softly and politely. He noticed the guitar hanging on the wall and asked which one of us was the player. "Nobody plays it," said the mess boy. "It's defective."

"Would you mind if I give it a try?" he asked.

The mess boy shrugged his shoulders: "I don't care."

The electrician took it off the wall, looked it over, tightened the chords, and struck a few notes. "Sounds okay," he said, then proceeded to play *Anțonio Barka.* After that he played *Malaguena* and, urged on by everyone who had gathered there, he played quite a few other Flamenco tunes. By then, crew members and officers had packed the lounge. We, the co-owners of the defective instrument, looked at each other and didn't utter a word.

*

The mystery of where we would unload our cargo of sugar was solved while transiting the Canal. The agent in Suez brought word that the ship would unload in New York, after making an intermediate stop in Pylos, Greece, for supplies. I, my cabinmate, and quite a few other crew members told the captain that we would be signing off in Greece. I had been on board the *Maritihi* for ten months; I wanted to get on a modern ship, preferably one with steam turbines, the propulsion engines of the future.

I had visited ships with that type of propulsion in the ports we had called, and I was impressed. Their engine rooms were clean and most of the lubrication was done by automatic lubricators instead of an oiler squirting the oil with an oilcan and getting his knuckles bruised by the crossheads. In some of the ships I visited, the accommodations were just as good as those of a nice hotel.

At the Maritime Academy, the professor teaching the course of Internal Combustion Engines seemed to be sure they were going to be the propulsion of the future, but I had visited some ships that had that kind of engine and didn't think much of them. The oiler of the twelve-to-four watch on the *Maritihi,* a heavy-set, slow-moving old-timer, had spent some time on a diesel-propelled ship and I had asked him what he thought of those engines.

"I spent six months on a British tramp that had a Doxford engine with opposing pistons," the old man told me. "It was the hardest six months I've spent anywhere. Every joint in that engine leaked. The whole engine room was covered in oil and exhaust soot. And when we got into port, as soon as we tied up and it rang: "Finished with engine", we started the repairs: change pistons, change rings, clean the turbocharges, resurface the valves, all kinds of ball-busting work. I didn't set foot on shore the whole time I was with that damn ship." I think it was his last comment that convinced me to look for ships with turbines for main propulsion.

During the evening watch, while standing under the ventilator, I asked Mastro Pandelis what he was going to do. He said he would continue the voyage. "There aren't many ships of this kind running anymore," he said. "Everything is modern and complicated nowadays, and nobody wants to hire an old fart like me. Anyway, I bet after unloading in New York we will load scrap iron from New Jersey for Japan, and they'll sell ship and cargo to some scrapper. That's what most companies have been doing with the Libertys lately." He paused and seemed to concentrate looking at the calendar above the engineer's desk. It was a calendar from a ship chandler in Vancouver that showed pastoral landscapes of Canada. The month of June was showing a large green field with a blue stream running in the middle and grey mountains at the distance. Mastro Pandelis seemed to study the picture.

"If they do sell her," he continued after a while, "I'll put in for my pension and help the son-in-law at the bakery in Volos. Maybe I'll teach the daughter how to cook *Ropa Vieha*." He took another look at the calendar, then went on: "I might even clear up the old homestead in the village and put in a vegetable garden. When I was young, we used to grow the best-tasting tomatoes there."

We arrived in Pylos on the sixth of June 1962. The Handris Shipping company brought the new crew on a chartered bus and took those who were signing off back to their office. For most of the day, the passageways and the mess halls were more crowded and noisier than an Arab market. People lugging seabags and suitcases were moving in every direction, old acquaintances greeting each other and exchanging news, and those who were leaving hurriedly briefing the newcomers on the idiosyncrasies of the ship. I was told my replacement would be arriving late and I never got to meet him.

I managed to fit all my clothes and the souvenirs into the same beat-up suitcase I had when I joined the ship. That prompted my cabinmate, Nikolas, to quip: "After all this time around crews from Hios, you still haven't picked up any of their self-promotion tricks."

"What do they do different?" I asked.

"When they come home from a long trip, they always bring lots of suitcases, even if they have one shirt and a pair of holey socks in each."

"Why they do a dumb thing like that?"

"So those who see them getting off the ferry in Hios, will spread word around the village that so-and-so's son came home and brought two donkey-loads of presents for his folks."

"Maybe I'll try it the next time," I said.

"I don't think so. You're not the type."

*

For a few days, I was a celebrity in Tsagarada. I bought drinks for everybody in the Bastounopoulos' coffee house, I thrilled the appreciative audience with my tales of fierce storms and exotic places and I assured my inquiring friends that the girls in Japan had slanted eyes but all the other parts of their anatomy were in the same location and of the same shape as the Greek girls. (I never mentioned my torment of the first crossing of the Indian Ocean.)

My father told me that Panagiotis Diamandeas had signed on a freighter in Piraeus one week after I did and got as far as Port Said. "From there, he wired home for the airfare back. He told his parents he was done with the sea," my father said with a chuckle. He took a puff on his cigarette then, while exhaling, asked, half seriously, half not, "How about you?"

"I'm in for the long haul," I said.

A few days after arriving in Greece, I applied for deferral from military service until I got the third engineer's license. That way, I could serve as an officer in the Navy.

CHAPTER SIX

It seems that government bureaucracy is neither quick nor simple in any country. Just like when I applied for the seaman's book, the military deferral application necessitated many trips between Athens and Volos. When the paperwork was finally approved, I returned to Piraeus to look for a ship. By then I knew something about shipping companies and opted to avoid those from the island of Hios. I had met some crewmembers from ships that belonged to Orion Shipping, and they told me that it was a good company to work for: The pay was decent, the food edible, and they treated everybody as normal people, even those who were from the mainland. Orion Shipping was founded by Mr. Goulandris who came from the island of Andros and, as I was to learn later, there was always a feud between these two islands. (Even now, the fastest way to piss off a captain from Hios or from Andros, is to tell him that a shipping company from the other island is a better employer.)

I decided to try my luck with Orion Shipping Company first and that proved to be a lucky choice. I was hired to go on the newest and largest ship of their fleet: the *Likaion*, a steam-turbine-propelled tanker due to arrive in Port Said in three days.

Having secured a job and having a little free time on my hands, I did some sightseeing. I spent half a day walking around the Acropolis and Parthenon then in the afternoon I took a bus to Sounion to see the temple of Poseidon. The next day I visited Nikolas, my cabinmate on the *Maritihi*, who lived in Piraeus, in a neighborhood called Taburia. Later, the two of us, and two of his friends went to dinner in a tavern by a small square, not far from his home. We ordered calamari for appetizers and a carafe of wine and talked about our time on board our old ship. When the waiter brought a big tray of fried calamari and a basket of bread, it prompted Nikolas to tell his friends about the shark the bosun caught off the coast of the Philippines, and the captain made the cook serve it for dinner. That surprised his friends who had never been abroad. "Next thing, you'll be telling us they fed you turtle meat," said one of them.

"No, that would be too expensive for our cheapskate captain," said Nikolas. "In most parts of the world that's considered a delicacy. It was on the menu of that fancy restaurant in Colombo, you remember?" he asked me.

"Yes, I remember," I said. "Over there they'll eat turtle, but they won't eat bread." Then while I was passing around the basket with sliced, warm Greek bread, Nikolas told them what happened at that fancy restaurant in Colombo. "And their bread, was nothing like this," he concluded.

His friends seemed to be more astounded that there were people in the world who would eat a whole meal without bread than when he told them about having shark meat for dinner. To the non-Greeks who are probably perplexed about the importance we place on eating bread, especially in the old days, before the health gurus took the joy out of breaking a freshly baked loaf of bread and munching on it, I would like to point out that bread is considered the most basic of foods in our country. So much so, that when Greeks talk about the shape of the economy, the price of a loaf of bread is used as a gauge. It's not unusual to hear one say: "Things are getting tough, bread shot up another half a drachma a loaf."

I asked Nikolas how he made out with the stones he bought in Colombo and said he sold them for a good profit to a jeweler friend. He showed me the ring he had made from a blue stone he kept. It was pretty.

I left Athens on the fifteenth of July 1962. This time the company flew me to Alexandria, Egypt, and I joined the ship in Port Said, on her way to load in the Persian Gulf. The captain of the launch pointed her to me in the distance, anchored and empty, waiting to join the convoy east. At that moment, her smokestack was belching plumes of thick black smoke that drifted slowly up towards the clouds.

"She's as big as a mountain," I said.

"Yes, she is," he chortled, "with a volcano on the top." He maneuvered the launch alongside the gangway, then tied my suitcase to a heaving line somebody threw from above and I started climbing a long ladder. I looked up and it seemed the end was disappearing among the clouds. This ship was five times larger than *Maritihi*.

After signing the papers at the captain's office, the steward showed me to my cabin, a paneled room, all my own. "Dinner is being served now," he said. "The kitchen will close in an hour." I told him I wasn't hungry. I dropped my suitcase and without bothering to change my shore clothes, I went down below to look at the engine room.

I found the first assistant in the boiler room fussing at the fireman about not watching his fuel temperature and letting the boilers smoke. The First was a short, slim man between thirty and forty, with curly brown hair and a thin mustache. He seemed to take notice of my skinny frame. "Glad to see we got somebody that'll fit through the manholes," he said as we shook hands. "You'll be on the eight-to-twelve watch for now. I'll get the twelve-to-four cadet to show you around." He hailed a chubby fellow about my age working on a boiler sight glass a few feet away, introduced us, and told him to show me what I would be doing.

My tour guide's name was Giannis. He had graduated from a Maritime Academy in Piraeus and had been on *Likaion* almost a year. Now he was getting ready for the third engineer's examination, he said. He started by showing me the main instrument panel with all the important pressure gauges and thermometers and the two large maneuvering wheels: the white one for AHEAD and the red for ASTERN. To the left of the panel was a box-like soundproof cubicle with the telephone inside.

The steering gear and most of the pumps were driven by electric motors, "Just open the valves and flip the switch," said Giannis. "There is a full-time marine electrician on board that takes care of everything electric. He's the equivalent of third engineer and works under the first."

I asked him about the Third that would be on my watch: "What kind of a guy is he?"

"He's an easy-going fellow," he said, "and so is everyone else, except the chief engineer."

"What about the chief?" I asked.

"The *Admiral*, signed on last month," said Giannis. "This is his first ship after he retired from the Navy and runs everything as if he were still on his frigate. Just do your chores and try to stay out of his way. The only time you'll see him is when you take the fuel readings and the propeller revolutions to his office."

"Was he really an admiral? Do I have to salute him?"

"He wasn't an admiral and, no, we don't salute him, although he probably would like us to." He started toward the stairs. "Come, I'll show you the steering gear."

On the upper platform, I paused and took it all in: The engine room was huge and clean. Every pipe was painted a different color, depending on what it was carrying—yellow for lubricating oil, blue for fresh water, green for salt water, and so on. Every piece of machinery was the latest of its kind, equipped with automatic lubricators and speed-control mechanisms. No more bruised knuckles trying to get a few drops of oil in the piston cross pins and no more wrestling with obstinate butterfly valves. All the engine cadets had to do was walk around and make sure the pressures and temperatures of all machinery were what they were supposed to be, and that the bilges were pumped. I had hit the jackpot in a big way!

"What kind of ports do you usually go to?" I asked.

"Persian Gulf to America and Rotterdam mostly." He opened the door to the steering gear room. "Sometimes we go somewhere else. I wish we would make more trips like the last one."

"Where was that?" I asked.

"In Tenerife, in the Canaries. It was a small terminal and could only receive at half pressure. It took us seven whole days to unload. It was the longest we've stayed in any port."

That last part of his answer gave a swift kick to my high-flying spirits, and my belief that I had hit the jackpot *big time*, took a nosedive. Then it continued spiraling downward as Giannis kept talking. "Usually, we stay about two days at the loading port and about three days when we discharge. That's our average stay in any port when things are normal."

That was the first shock I got on my new ship. The second, bigger than the first, came later, when I saw the kind of ports we were loading from and the ones we were discharging to.

In the evening, about five hours after I signed on, we got ready to transit the Suez Canal. The line handling crew descended upon us, and we took our place in the convoy behind a Norwegian bulk carrier and ahead of a Liberty-type freighter that made me think of the *Maritihi*, and Mastro Pandelis and I wondered where they were now.

During the watch, the third engineer asked me if I made sure the porthole and the door of my cabin were locked. "If you haven't, you'll find an empty cabin when you get back," he said.

"This is the third time I'm crossing the Canal," I said.

"Just the same, be careful, they're very sneaky. I just watched one of the line handlers on deck. He was talking to our bosun, and while doing that, he kept unscrewing with his heel the brass cap of the sounding tube for the water tank; these guys can steal your pants while you're wearing them and you won't know it until you feel the breeze on your ass."

After we got through the Suez Canal we headed for Mina Al-Ahmadi, in the Persian Gulf. "That's the best of all the ports we've been loading from," Giannis said when he relieved me at the midnight watch. "Sometimes we go to Um Said or to Ras Tanura, they're all the same, but Mina Al-Ahmadi has a seaman's club that's air-conditioned."

When we entered the Gulf of Oman, we had to shut the starboard boiler down because a tube developed a leak. We proceeded at reduced speed toward the loading port while waiting for the boiler to cool off so we could go inside and plug the tube.

"You're in luck," the First joked, "You get to go inside with me. You're the only cadet who can get through the manholes."

We entered the boiler twelve hours after we had shut it down. It was still stifling hot but the First said he would give it a try and I had to follow him in. It took over five hours to locate the leaky tube and put a plug on both ends of it.

While we were inside the boiler the first and I were the stars of the engine crew. Outside, crowding near the boiler manholes, was quite a gathering, even the *admiral* was there, handing us tools and cold lemonade while continuously pouring out pep-talk words.

The good ship *Likaion* limped into Mina Al-Ahmadi oil terminal during the twelve-to-four watch, soon after we finished with the boiler repairs. I was dead-tired but for a while, I fought off the urge to go to bed and after gulping my lunch I went on the deck for a better view. I wanted to have a look at what the loading ports of my new ship looked like. All I could see were rows and rows of huge, round, white petrol-storage tanks, and a maze of pipes and manifolds. Some of the pipes extended out to the mile-long pier that our ship was tying up to. The air had a sour, sulfury smell and was just as hot as the inside of the starboard boiler.

"Is this the town?" I asked the cook's assistant standing next to me.

"They say there is a town a few miles farther inland," he said.

I shielded my eyes and looked inland, but all I could see were sand dunes and more sand dunes. This place made even Marmagoa look like paradise.

The instant the last mooring line was secured, four hoists with black hoses dangling like elephant tusks swung over from the dock and were connected to our cargo manifold. Moments later, I saw the pumpman dive into the abyss of the pump room and soon after I heard the thumping sound of the ballast pumps. Deckhands were dashing about, opening certain valves, and closing others as the ballast was sent ashore and the cargo poured into the belly of our ship.

"We'll be casting off about this time tomorrow," said the cook's helper, wiping the sweat with his apron.

"Are all the places we go like this?" I asked.

"No, some have different color tanks," said the cook's helper with a chuckle as he turned around. "I'll take this apron off and go to the club and get a cold drink."

"Where is the Seamen's Club?"

"Right over there." He pointed to a structure on pilings at the end of the pier.

"You mean that shack?"

"It has air-conditioning," he said and walked away.

I went to my cabin; I had seen enough. It was nothing like the ports-of-call of the good-old *Maritihi*, where the main part of the town, with the shops and the seamen's entertainment establishments, were only a few yards from the docks.

At that time of day my cabin was almost the same temperature as the outside. The only attempt at comfort was through a feeble, bulkhead-mounted fan which only moved the hot air around. When at sea, we would place a vent cowl, a scoop-like air receiver, in the porthole that would bring in some fresh air, but here we didn't dare open the portholes because the desert sand would come rushing in. This time I was tired enough to ignore all the discomforts and just lay down. I think I was asleep before I hit the bed.

The banging on the door woke me up from a lethargic sleep. "Skandza Vardia" (watch change), the gravelly voice of the four-to-eight cadet informed. I had slept six hours straight. He stood by the door to make sure I got out of bed. "You're sweating a river," he said. "A couple more drops and you'll be floating."

When my watch was over, I took a quick shower and walked along the pier and up the wooden steps to the Seamen's Club. The cool, refreshing breeze from the air-conditioning hit me in the face the moment I opened the door. Almost every chair in the place was occupied by men from our crew and the Oriental crew of the ship behind us. Most of them were dozing off holding a half-empty soda-bottle in their hand. At the counter, four Arabs in white djellabas were having an animated discussion. I ordered an orange soda and joined some of our men at a table. There was not much conversation going on and the few sentences uttered every now and then had to do with trying to guess what the discharging port would be. We prolonged our stay in that place as long as we could, then, as we were leaving, each one of us repeated the same words: "Wish I could carry some of this coolness in my pockets."

Just as the assistant cook predicted, we departed in the afternoon of the next day. It was announced that this time we would go to Rotterdam again to discharge and on the way there we would stop at the Skaramanga Shipyard, in Piraeus, for minor repairs.

My friend Giannis, the two third engineers, the first assistant, and many others seized the opportunity to sign off. The chief engineer fired the other cadet, and in the end, the *admiral* and I were the only ones left from the old engine crew.

It didn't take the shipyard long to do the repairs the office wanted and forty-eight hours later we were ready to go. The day we were scheduled to depart, I was called to the captain's office. I got there as fast as I could; being asked to report to the captain's office is usually connected with bad news. "I've been informed by these gentlemen," the captain said when I got there, "that I must sign you off." He was nodding toward the side-table, where two men from the Coast Guard were sipping coffee. "They say you have to report to the Army."

"But I've got a deferral, I showed you the paper, Captain," I said.

"They say it was a clerical error, the deferral should not have been issued, I'm sorry," he said.

I went to the first assistant and told him that I would be leaving also. He had signed on a few hours earlier and was in the middle of unpacking. Right then he was holding a hanger with a white jacket with gold stripes on it. He turned around and looked at me, and his face had a look of bewilderment.

"Why did you wait until now?" he asked. I told him why and he seemed to be thinking for a while. "Come with me," he said afterward.

I followed him to the chief engineer's office. He walked in without knocking. The chief was talking to the steward at the time. "Nick," said the First, "I have a problem. The Coast Guard wants to take him out."

He pointed to me. I was standing behind him, recovering from the shock that he dared to interrupt the *Admiral's* conversation and called him by his first name. "They say he needs to report to the Army. His deferral was a *clerical error,* they say."

The chief looked at me.

"I got deferral till I got my Third's license and then …"

"The thing is," the first cut me off, "he's the only one from the old crew; you've fired the rest. He's the only one who knows where anything is, I just got on board. It'll be like it was in the frigate *Poseidon* all over again. I need him to...

"Go back to what you were doing," the chief said to me, "I'll take care of it; you're staying on board."

"Yes, sir. Thank you very much, sir," I said and went out.

Soon after we sailed for Rotterdam. The bridge cadet told me we would be there in ten days. I looked forward to some excitement that would make up for the dullness of the Persian Gulf. I had heard many stories from those who had been there about the different places the Dutch had to entertain salt-crusted mariners.

We picked up the pilot during the twelve-to-four watch and, after a quick lunch, I dashed on deck to look at the new port. Another disappointment. All I could see was a forest of pipes and storage tanks. Those who had been there before said I would need to take an oil-company shuttle bus to the main gate and, from there, a taxi to the part of town where the excitement was.

"The *entertainment girls* sit in display windows like mannequins in clothing stores, each advertising their best parts," a deckhand told me. "You can walk up and down the street, look them over and get your pick. Every time I come here that's the first place I go. You're going to like it, I'm sure."

As it turned out I didn't get to do any of that. As soon as the ship was tied up, they hooked up the hoses for discharging and I had to stand an extra watch on the cargo pumps. There were four turbine-driven machines that got started the moment the deckhands finished hooking up the hoses to the cargo manifold.

We finished the discharging and the ballasting in forty-eight hours, and we were off again to the Persian Gulf. The fireman on my watch had made the trip to town and later, during our watch, every moment I got close to him in the engine room he would relate in vivid colors the fun he had in the red-light district.

"Next trip I'm going ashore, no matter what," I said. "I'll trade my watch with somebody if I have to." As it turned out, the ship did not make another trip there during the time I was onboard. (I did eventually go to Rotterdam and to Amsterdam. It was about forty years later as a tourist, with my wife. By then my bucket list had undergone a complete re-arrangement and red-light districts of any port had been tossed out.)

At lunchtime, the day after we left Rotterdam, the helmsman coming down from the bridge announced that he heard the chief mate say the ship got a long-term charter to carry oil for Chevron Oil Company from the Persian Gulf to United States.

"Damn," mocked the oiler across the table from me. "I'll have to press my djellaba for the ball in Mina Al-Ahmadi."

"You're in luck, you won't even have to take a shower," countered the deckhand. "This time we're loading in Ras Tanura, where we pick up the hoses from a buoy, two miles from the shore. We'll be enjoying the panoramic view of the sand dunes with the binoculars. Oh, I forgot, you don't have complicated tools like that in the engine room."

The loading terminal in Ras Tanura was just like the deckhand had described it. We picked up the cargo hoses from a buoy about two miles away from the sand dunes and twenty-four hours later we headed for San Pedro in the United States. We arrived in California thirty days later. We picked up another buoy with hoses attached to it and started discharging. We could see the town far away, but only the captain and those who needed to see a doctor could take the launch to go ashore.

"We draw too much water to go alongside," the fireman on my watch told me. "Sometimes, if they need the grade of cargo we have, we'll discharge half of it at anchorage and then they'll move us to a dock at the refinery to unload the rest."

"How far is the town from there?" I asked him.

"They told me it's not far from there. There is a bus stop near the main gate, next to a sailor bar. We don't stay more than twelve hours on that dock, so I never went any farther than the bar. I heard we will be going alongside on this trip," he said.

We docked at the beginning of my shift. After my regular watch, all I had time to do was visit the sailor bar across the street from the main gate. Its real name was, "The Home Away from Home," painted in gold letters on a wooden sign that was made to look like the stern of an old frigate. Below the sign was a large picture of a Hollywood-style sailor, tall and weathered, in a peacoat, with a cap, and a seabag over his shoulder. It seems there were too many English words in the name to remember, so when the men on the ship talked about it, they referred to it as "the sailor bar."

There was only time for one beer and a quick appraisal of the girls working in the entertainment field, all of whom, as it turned out, were too expensive for my pay. After that, I dashed back on board to relieve the man on watch on the cargo pumps, cursing on the way my rotten luck for getting me a job on this floating jail. The time on the *Maritihi*, where, at every port we went, we stayed for weeks, had spoiled me. This hummingbird-style port of calls was becoming hard to get used to.

We proceeded toward the Persian Gulf at economic speed, which meant Chevron Oil wasn't in a hurry for another load. As we were approaching the Hawaiian Islands, the chief steward got sick and lay in his bed with strong intestinal pains. The radio operator kept asking for medical advice from anywhere he could get a response and passed it on to the chief mate, but whatever they tried it didn't seem to bring any relief to the patient. When we got close to Honolulu, we were boarded by a team of the American Coast Guard that had a medical person with them. After examining the steward, they said he needed to be taken to the hospital. The bosun lowered him with the provisioning hoist in a stretcher into the Coast Guard launch and they took him with them.

For a while, that incident provided conversation material and a reason for reminiscing by the old-timers of the crew, when we sat under the canopy of the poop-deck in the evenings as our ship headed towards the furnace of the Percian Gulf at her economic speed.

*

The loading terminal in Ras Tanura with all its thrills and excitement was waiting for us. We picked up the cargo hoses from the same buoy, about two miles away from the sand dunes, and twenty-four hours later we headed back to where we had come from.

During the voyage, every now and then one of my lower back teeth would shoot a sharp pain for a few seconds then go away. It didn't last long so I kept ignoring it but soon after we left Ras Tanura, that tooth started shooting pain more often and this time it was lasting longer. I went to the chief mate, who gave me some pills to take whenever it happened, and that seemed to have solved the problem. Then the day before arriving in San Pedro, in California, while I was going about my chores during my morning watch, I took a bite on a hard apple I had gotten from the pantry earlier and immediately felt a sharp stab of pain running through my lower jaw. I spat out the piece of apple, and with it, half of my back tooth.

I took a handful of the chief mate's pills and told the first assistant that I needed to go to the dentist in San Pedro. He said he'd ask the other cadets to cover my watch, if needed.

We arrived at the anchorage at sunrise. By the time the customs and the immigration inspection were over, and the yellow flag came down, those of us going to the doctor were lined up outside the officer's smoking room. Besides me there was a deckhand who had hurt his shoulder when he fell from a scaffold two days earlier, and the cook who had been complaining about a pain in his belly.

We boarded the launch at eleven thirty. I was glad for the chance to see some of the country besides the sailor bar, even if it was a painful way to do it. The man driving the agency van that took us to the doctor spoke Greek with an Athenian accent. When we got on the road, he told us his name was Leonidas Karagiorgis and asked what part of Greece we came from. The cook and the deckhand were from Korthio, a village on the island of Andros.

"Never heard of it," said the driver. He hadn't heard of Tsagarada either, so I explained it was a village outside Volos. "Yeah, I heard of Volos," he said. "It's a small town about half a day's drive north of Athens, isn't it?"

"Yes, it is," I said. "Where do *you* come from?"

"I was born and raised in Athens," he said. "Did some sailing for a few years, but it didn't take me long to figure out that kind of life wasn't for me. I like living in a big city. And I like to have some fun at the end of my workday. I stayed ashore and I've been helping the agent run the business; I handle all the Greek ships. He doesn't make a move without checking with me first."

"How big is this town?" I asked.

"San Pedro is a big city. Three times bigger than Athens," he said. Then suddenly he slammed the wheel: "Oh, shit!"

"What happened?" we asked.

"You kept talking to me, and I missed the exit. Now I've got to go two miles out of my way."

"Why is that?" I asked him.

"Man, this is a big city," he said, "with lots of cars on the road. We are in what we call here a *freeway*; it's not the little goat-path of your village. I must change lanes and get off at the next exit. It's two miles up ahead from here, damn it!"

There were indeed lots of cars on the road. I had been looking out of the window since we got in the van, and I was awed at the amount of traffic. The freeway we were on had four lanes full of bumper-to-bumper vehicles of every kind, all of them going in the direction we were going. And there was another river like it on the other side of the four lanes, going in the opposite direction; I felt like a frog riding on a log in a metallic river. I had never seen anything like it.

At the medical building, the driver told me I would have to wait in the lobby. "I have to go with these two to do the translating for them," he said in a way of explanation.

"You go with him to the dentist," snapped the cook. "Us two can take care of ourselves. I spent five years in Australia, don't need a smart aleck from Athens to do the translating for me."

The driver didn't answer. He walked to the receptionist desk and talked with the person behind it for a few minutes, then came back and told the cook that the nurse would come to take them to the X-Ray room shortly, and after that, to the doctor.

"Wait for us here when you finish," he said. "I'm taking him to the dentist, on the next floor." Then he motioned for me to follow him.

We had to wait for a while for the doctor to see me, and during the conversation, the man from the agency told me that he had seen the ship's charter for the next six months. "You're scheduled to make three more trips like this," he said.

Suddenly I felt as if a dam deep inside me had burst and a gusher of curses headed toward my throat. I had been nursing the hope that perhaps the ship would make another trip to Rotterdam where I could get to see the street with the interesting window decorations or even a trip to the Canary Islands where they took a week to unload. To be told in plain, cold words that for almost six more months I would be subjected to the same monastic existence as the last two, it was too much my adventure-seeking brain could tolerate.

I swallowed, coughed a couple of times and faking joy as best as I could, said, "That's good, maybe you can show us around the next time we're here."

Soon after, a nurse ushered us to the doctor's chair. The doctor looked into my mouth and after some poking and mumbling and the driver translating, took out what was left of my tooth.

Not long after, the man from the agency took me and the deckhand back to the ship. He said the cook had to be admitted to the hospital for more tests. "Hope they let him out before we leave," said the deckhand. "His helper can't even boil water."

For the rest of the day, it felt like saliva was constantly running down my chin and I kept wiping my face. A few hours after we got back, during my evening watch, the ship was moved to the pier to unload the remaining cargo.

*

There have been multitudes of stories written about people's lives altered, and about brutal crimes committed, and complex mysteries solved, based on someone's habit of talking too much. As I write this, I can't help stopping to stare out of the window and ponder how my life would have evolved if the man from the shipping agency hadn't said that the ship was scheduled for three more trips identical to the one we had just completed. I would have probably stayed on board, hoping we would make another trip to Tenerife, or perhaps a similar port, where we could stay a whole week. Giannis had told me that a few months earlier the ship went to Marcelles and in the middle of the unloading, the longshoremen's union had called for a strike, and they ended up staying four extra days alongside the dock. I would probably have used my time of forced frugal behavior to prepare myself for the third engineer's examinations, then join the Navy, and after that, who knows.

I was not planning to jump ship in America, nor anywhere else for that matter. My long-range plans at that time were to see as much of the world as I could, then retire to some small seaside village in England and spend my days taking long walks along the white cliffs of Dover and occasional trips to my village in Greece, during the summer. (I had been reading lots of Dickens and Cronin at the time.)

But having to make three more trips on the *Likaion* and doing nothing more exciting than seeing sand dunes, storage tanks, and sea buoys, meant half a year of my life. A few days earlier I had my twenty-first birthday, time was marching on!

By the end of my second watch, I had made my decision. I didn't share my thoughts with anyone, and I didn't ask for advice from anyone. Unlike my previous ship where there was a closeness among all the crew members, of the engine and deck departments alike, on the *Likaion*, at least as far as I could tell, everybody kept to themselves. After Giannis, the engine cadet of the twelve-to-four watch disembarked in Piraeus, I didn't develop any close friendships with any of the crew. Apart from the Admiral, all others of the engine crew had joined the ship in Piraeus two months earlier and, perhaps, it was not enough time to develop bonding friendships. The third engineer on my watch was a nice, mild-mannered man about thirty years old, by the name of Mastro Mitsos. During quiet moments of our shift, we used to talk about steam turbines and diesel engines and even about life, but we never ventured inside each other's thoughts.

When my evening eight-to-twelve shift was over, I cleaned up and walked to the gate of the terminal. To the crewmembers I ran into on the way, I said I was going to the sailor bar planning on having some *serious* fun.

At the security guard station, I showed my pass to the man on duty, and he wrote my name on the "OUT" column of a book-page with my ship's name on the top. Then I walked to the bus stop and went into town and got a room at the first hotel I came across. It was about one o'clock in the morning. The ship was supposed to sail at sunrise.

It was Thursday, November 29, 1962. I had been on board the *Likaion* four and a half months.

*

Although I planned to sleep late, I woke up early the next day and had to force myself to stay in bed. When I couldn't keep myself in bed any longer, I got up and went to the hotel cafeteria. After breakfast I walked around, mostly browsing in the aisles of a grocery store close to the hotel. I was amazed at the plethora and the variety of eatable things packaged in cans, bottles, and multicolored boxes stacked on the shelves. I wondered how the owner of the store could remember all the things he had in the place. I was also amazed at the way they were selling the things. In Greece, you walked into the store, told the person in the front what you wanted, and they would get it for you while you waited. Here, people walked through the aisles, filling up a pushcart or a basket, then took it to the cashier by the entrance and paid the price that was on the sticker. At the time I thought it was a naive way to run a store. In Greece, a store like this would probably go broke before they finished opening the doors. The stuff would be pouring out, inside deep pockets and under overcoats, faster than they could put it on the shelves. (Later visits to Greece proved how far off the mark my thoughts were at the time.)

Around noon I took the bus that went by the docks. The road ran parallel to the water and from my window seat I could see at the distance the ship still tied to the pier. I wondered if they had problems with the cargo pumps. If they did, the engineers would be busy right now and I should have been there. I got up to pull the cord for the stop but quickly changed my mind and sat back down.

I got off the bus two stops past the port entrance. At the nearest bar, I ordered whiskey, and before the bartender asked for it, I put my boarding pass on the counter.

"Straight?" he asked after glancing at my boarding pass. His voice had more of a bewilderment than a question mark in it. I nodded. I took a sip and tried to slosh some inside my mouth, but it stung where the tooth had come out, and I almost screamed. At the far end of the counter a tormented-looking man said something and toasted me with his beer. The only words I understood out of what he said was "fuck" and "damn." I pretended to be absorbed examining the bottom of my whisky glass and didn't answer; I was afraid he might want to start a conversation.

When the bartender wasn't looking, I dipped my fingers in the glass and rubbed some of the whiskey around my neck. I also spilled a little on my shirt. Soon after, I got out and boarded the bus to the docks. This time the ship was gone. I pulled the cord, got off, and ran to the gate. I showed my pass to one of the two guards and in fluent Greek I asked them where my ship was. The man who read the name on the pass told me the ship had left almost one hour ago. I pretended I didn't understand him.

"*LIKAION, LIKAION, pou ine* (where is) *LIKAION?"* I kept repeating. The two guards talked to each other for a few minutes and then one of them made a phone call. Soon after, two more immigration people came, but neither one of them spoke Greek, so I kept on repeating: "I no spit English, *LIKAION, pou ine to LIKAION*?" One of the immigration men who seemed to be the supervisor of the group started making telephone calls and on the fourth call, he handed me the receiver. The person on the other end asked me in Greek what happened. I thought I recognized the voice of the man who drove the agency van. I told him that last night, I met a girl at the sailor bar, and she took me to a hotel. When I woke up, she was gone, and when I tried to get back to the ship, I took the wrong bus. That's why I was late. Then I passed the phone to the immigration man, and I guess the Greek from the agency repeated what I had told him. When he hung up, he gestured for me to get in their car, and they took me to their office. The Greek from the shipping agency was there also. They asked me again what had happened, and I repeated the story one more time.

One of the men was writing everything down on a typewriter as fast as the agency man translated it and, every so often he would tell him to slow down. "Can't keep up with you, buddy."

When they finished with their questions, the policeman doing the typing straightened his papers, put them in a file, and got up. Walking away he turned toward the interpreter: "Tell him that the sailor bar is a bad place. He's lucky he didn't get mugged or worse." The Greek translated it, and I just nodded in agreement.

They made more phone calls and talked among themselves some more and finally, the Greek, sounding very official informed me: "The agent has to talk to the personnel man in New York, but they're already closed for the day and can't reach him; they're three hours ahead of us you know?" He faced the immigration men and sounding as if speaking to comrades he said: "In America, we no stay in office after five o'clock on Fridays, eh?"

"Some of us do it, buddy," answered one of the men, but the Greek acted as if he hadn't heard him.

Facing me while tapping on his wristwatch he said slowly, as if speaking to a toddler: "It's now six o'clock over there. Tomorrow it is Saturday. It will be Monday before the agent knows something. I'm going to take you to a hotel until they will decide what to do with you."

On the way to the hotel, the man from the agency asked me if I wanted to stay in America. "I can arrange it for you," he said, in a conspiratorial tone of voice. "It won't cost you much."

I wasn't ready to stay ashore and settle down in America or anywhere else, I wanted to travel and see the world, but I was curious how the Greek from the agency would arrange it. "How much will I have to pay to stay here?" I asked him.

"No more than two thousand dollars," he said. "You pay one thousand in the beginning, and the rest you can pay it little by little." I stared out of the window, looking like I was thinking.

"I know a woman," he went on, "who, for one thousand dollars, will marry you and after you get the green card, she will give you a divorce. You, being an engineer, will have no trouble getting a job and making top dollar as we say here. You'll pay me off and will be driving a fancy car with a hot girlfriend next to you in no time."

"Sounds good," I said. "The problem is, I only have on me what's left of the fifty dollars I drew from the captain when I went ashore; it's a good thing the girl last night didn't take my wallet. I have more coming to me from the ship. If you give me your number, I'll call you as soon as I get paid off."

He didn't answer. He seemed to be concentrating on reading the street names. Then he pulled into a driveway and stopped under a sign that read, "Howard Johnson's Inn."

"That's it, your hotel," he said. He got out and motioned with his head for me to follow. We went in and he walked up to the registration and told the middle-aged lady behind the counter that he was from the agency. She said somebody from there had already called and made the arrangements. She gave him a key, and my driver said he'd show me the room. He unlocked the door, stepped inside and looked around as if making sure there was nobody in there.

"You're all set," he said afterward. He handed me the key and a card. "Think of what we talked about earlier. This is your chance. My private number is on the back of this card."

I read the card, SAMUELSON SHIPPING AGENCY, with the street address and a phone number. On the back, written in the handwriting of someone who hadn't done much handwriting, was, "Leo Kar" and a phone number, different than the one on the front.

"They know me as Leo in the office, like the lion," he said cracking a smile that showed a row of brown teeth. "I'm independent, I do special jobs for the agents and the ship chandlers." As he walked away, he added, "I'll come by Monday to check on you. Enjoy your vacation."

I knew about these kinds of independent entrepreneurs; they seemed to be in every port. In the Greek maritime parlance, they were called *Bitsikomides*, which I found out later is derived from the English "beachcombers." They survived by mooching on seamen, running errands, and doing special jobs for anybody having anything to do with the waterfront. I assured him I would be thinking of his proposition.

*

I had heard on the ship that Hollywood, where they made all of the cowboy movies, wasn't far from San Pedro. I wondered if I could take a trip there and walk around the town, maybe I would see some of the movie stars, like Jeff Chandler or John Wayne.

On Saturday morning I asked the lady behind the reception desk how to get to Hollywood. She tried to explain, but I didn't understand even half of her instructions, so I said, "Thank you," and, not daring to venture too far, I took a walk near the hotel instead. Later that day, two Greek-speaking men about my age came and asked the receptionist something, then went and sat on a couch in the lobby. I approached them and asked if they were in the movies. They thought it was funny and laughed. I asked them how far Hollywood was and how to get there. They said a couple of sentences in English to each other, fast, and in a way that made me think they didn't want me to understand. Then one of them asked me why I wanted to go there.

"Just wanted to see where they make the movies, and maybe even see some of the movie stars, like Jeff Chandler, or John Wayne," I said.

They laughed and again, spoke to each other in fast English again, and then one of them asked me what part of Greece I was from. I told him and after I clarified it was a village outside Volos, I thought I saw something like a smirk on his face. “It’s too far away, and too hard for you to get there,” he said. “You’ll end up in Mexico.” Then he started talking to his partner in English about something, acting as if I wasn’t there.

I walked out and went for another stroll.

I spent my vacation wandering not farther than a few blocks from the hotel and browsing in a supermarket. As I write this, I’m amazed at how fascinated I was at the time with the American supermarkets and the people shopping in them, most of whom were women in tight shorts and revealing halters. I picked up a can of peaches and a can of pears—they were luxury items on the ship—and, copying the person ahead of me, I gave an elderly lady at the cash register near the door a five-dollar bill. When she gave me the change she told me to have a nice day.

I remember wondering if anyone ever walked out without paying.

On Monday morning the Greek from the agency was knocking on my door. “I came to take you to the airport,” he said. “It looks like they are going to send you on a ship in the East Coast.” He drove me to the airport and stayed with me until it was boarding time, to make sure I got on the right plane to New York, he said.

This time the flight was much longer than the one from Athens to Alexandria, about three times longer. While we were in the air, they served everyone drinks and even a meal. I looked out of the window and remember thinking: *all these hours of flying and we’re still in the same country.*

When we got to New York, a man from the Orion Shipping Company met me and took me to the Hotel Rex on Forty-Seventh Street, in Manhattan. He said he would be back the next day to take me to my ship that was coming to unload in New Haven. “It’s about four hours from here,” he said.

There were a few Greek-speaking people in the hotel lobby watching a cowboy show on television, but I was too tired to socialize and went straight to my room. (In the years that followed I spent a lot of time watching television and socializing in the lobby of the Hotel Rex.)

From the drive through the snow-covered countryside to New Haven, all I remember was that the person from Orion Shipping, a mild-mannered, thin, gray-haired man, was constantly looking at his map and asking for directions at the toll booths of the highway. Then when we arrived, I remember, he had to park away from the ship, and we walked a long way on a street with dirty snow piled high on either side. In Dan Pedro, in order to make it believable that I missed the ship by accident, I had gone ashore dressed for California weather: a short-sleeved shirt and no undershirt. Now I was shivering. I kept my hands in my pockets, as deep as I could get them and trying to convince myself it was not really that cold.

Fortunately, a Greek selling used clothes had come on board when the ship docked and set up shop in the crew's lounge. He had all kinds of men's clothes, all of them used, except the underwear and socks which were new. The captain was a reasonable kind of man and let me have a small advance; enough to buy a couple of changes of clothes.

As I found out later, there were many people, all along the coast of the United States, who came on the ships and sold clothes like he did. Most of those merchants were ex-seamen who after sailing for some years, got married and stayed ashore. It seemed to be a profitable kind of business.

CHAPTER SEVEN

My new ship was the tanker, *Andros Sea*. She was one-third the size of the *Likaion*. When I signed on board I was put on the eight-to-twelve watch. One of the cadets told me that the ship was primarily trading in the Caribbean and the east coast of the American continent. "We go to the United States, South America, and sometimes to Europe," he said. That sounded a lot better than the itinerary of the ship I had just left.

The captain told me he had instructions from the office to deduct the money the company spent on me for missing the ship in San Diego. "I'll be taking it out a little every pay period, so it won't seem so bad," he said. It seemed the "taking out a little every pay period" lasted a very, very long time.

We departed New Haven two days after I got on board. From there, we went to Sint Nicolaas, in Aruba where we loaded Bunker C for Freeport in Grand Bahama. Sint Nicolaas was one of the most popular ports for the merchant seamen of any country. Bars of any style and nationality and their affiliated *pleasure palaces* lined up right outside the harbor gate, on *Zeppanfedstraat* Street, and on the secondary streets around it. And, like the songs of sirens, jukeboxes blared in many languages, the latest popular tunes, beckoning the sailors into their embrace.

My first Christmas in a tropical place was different from all my previous Christmases. It was a hot, windless day, and the ship had been at anchor, in Freeport for three days. Two days earlier, the bosun brought on board a green bush he cut near the docks, and with the help of the messboy, he set it up in the crew's lounge. It was a scraggly-looking, broad-leafed, tropical bush which, after a lot of clipping and trimming, was brought into a somewhat conical shape. On top, they put a star, made of cardboard and tin foil. They talked the chief mate into donating some cotton from the first aid supplies and placed it carefully on the branches. I and Drakos, the fireman of my watch, happen to be passing by on our way to the engine room and paused to watch them decorate it. At the time, the mess boy was agonizing over spreading the snow evenly on the branches and that prompted Drakos to quip, "Don't be so fussy, it looks real; I'm getting chills just standing next to it."

The electrician, who was a talented amateur painter, painted a smiling, life-size Santa Claus on a cardboard cutout and placed him next to the Christmas tree. In front of Santa, he put a large Bahamian straw basket, in such a way that looked like Santa was holding on to it. Then every one of the crew and the officers put a small gift in a gift-wrapped box in it. The electrician wrote numbers on them, and on Christmas Day, after the dinner and the caroling, sang by the entire crew, we drew a number from a bowl and were handed the corresponding gift box from Santa's basket. Everybody enjoyed the event, even the non-smokers who found cigars or a lighter in their gift box. Our captain, who was almost completely bald, got a tortoise shell comb.

"It's a good omen. It means I'm going to grow hair," he declared, and everyone laughed.

On New Year's Day we were again in Aruba, in Sint Nicolaas, loading Bunker C for Beaumont, Texas. It was a balmy, sunny day, and after lunch a couple of shipmates and I went for a walk around the town. On Rembrandt Street, in the front yards of many houses, people sat by tables loaded with food, pastries, and drinks, and passersby would stop and join them. They waved to us to come in, and we had cookies and drinks, and we wished each other, "Happy New Year," in Greek, English and Duch.

We arrived in Beaumont during my morning watch. As soon as it was over, Drakos asked me to go with him to help him make a phone call. He didn't even want to wait until I washed up. We told the mess boy to save our lunch and we headed toward the end of the dock.

"Never learned how to talk to those American telephone women," he said as we scurried toward the phone booth. "The wife of my youngest is supposed to have a baby. I hope this one is a boy, all I got up to now is granddaughters, need a boy to keep the family name alive."

At the booth, I gave the number to the operator and then fed the machine with coins out of the paper bag Drakos had brought. She connected me and I could hear the phone ringing at the other end. After a while, the operator said there was no answer.

I passed on the message to Drakos. "Tell her to let it ring," he said. "The phone is in the coffee house and it's probably too much noise."

I tried again and when finally, someone answered, I rushed to put more coins in and handed the receiver to Drakos. Then I stood outside the booth in case the operator asked to feed the machine some more. I could hear him shout to somebody at the other end for about a minute, then he hung up and stepped out of the booth looking tired.

"Well, did she have it?" I asked.

"It's a girl," he said. "She had it this morning. My boy was buying drinks for everybody in the coffee house. That's why they couldn't hear the phone ringing." We started walking toward the ship. "They're still young," he said, almost to himself. "This is their first one, they're going to try again, he promised."

"You should go home and see the new granddaughter," I said. "You've been on the ship for a long time. You've earned your ticket home and then some."

"I might do that in a couple of months, when the weather is better over there," he said.

"They tell me you keep saying that for over a year now."

He didn't answer. He opened his stride and kept a couple of steps ahead of me.

At the time Drakos had been on board for over two years. He took pride in knowing every quirkiness of every piece of machinery in the engine room and in being able to find his way around the boiler room even blindfolded. He could sense if something was out of norm way before it registered on the gauges. Some of us speculated that it might be the reason he didn't want to go home; he was afraid the company might send him on another ship afterward and he would have to learn everything all over again.

*

The *Andros Sea* was a good ship with a good crew. Most of the ports we called at were small towns where we usually stayed more than a few days. It gave me an opportunity to get a closer look at the people of the Caribbean islands and in the countries of the American continent. While with her, I visited practically every port in the Caribbean, some more interesting than others. Port of Spain, in Trinidad, was an interesting place. It was picturesque and we enjoyed the trips to town but there were still remnants of the old days when the island was a British colony. The first time we tried to go to the country club, which was the best and safest place for food and entertainment, some in our group were not allowed in because they were not officers. The next time our Chief Mate typed new passes for everyone and under occupation he listed deck or engine room cadet. When the receptionist said how come there were so many cadets on this ship, we said it was a training ship of the Hellenic Maritime Academy.

At the time, some of the behavior of the Americans seemed strange to me and to my European shipmates. I remember the time our ship was unloading in Beaumont, Texas. I and two other crewmembers, dressed in our colorful tropical outfits from Aruba, had been strolling along one of the main streets. It was soon after a short rain shower and we noticed an electrical transformer mounted on top of a wooden power pole was on fire. We thought we should tell somebody, and seeing no one on the street, I walked into a small bookstore and tried to tell an elderly lady that there was a fire in front of her store.

"See, fire," I said pointing upward. I don't know if it was my appearance or the way I said the English words, but she retreated toward the back of the store. I walked a few steps closer and repeated what I had said, but she walked back even more, and finally, she went and stood next to an old man behind the counter.

I realized they were afraid of me, and I went outside and stood at the edge of the sidewalk and kept repeating "See, fire," while pointing to the top of the pole. After a while, the elderly lady allowed half of her head, enough for one eye, to peek from behind the door. She saw the fire and immediately turned and shouted to the old man. "By Joe, there is a fire. Better call somebody." It was quite a contrast from the behavior of the people in Aruba a few days earlier.

Another time we happened to be laid up at a public pier in the Baltimore harbor, waiting on orders. Usually, in the evenings, those who weren't working or had gone ashore would sit in the stern under the canopy, telling stories while watching the stevedores on the adjacent piers go about their business. We always found something to compare the American workers with those of the other ports in the world; whether it was the way they zoomed around in the forklifts or the pace at which they worked or the clothes they wore.

One evening about five of us watched a man and a young boy fishing on the pier across from our ship. We were fascinated by the fishing gear the pair was using. The bosun, the most knowledgeable in our group, said that they were using a new kind of fishing pole. "Cane poles are out now; those over there are made with some kind of plastic, and they're flexible, see how they bend?"

He was right. At that moment the man was reeling in what must've been something big and his pole was bent to almost a complete circle. We walked closer to the bulwarks to get a better look at what he was bringing in. When it finally broke the surface, it turned out to be the loop-end of a broken mooring line, and we laughed. Soon after, the young boy cried out, "I got one, I got one," and started reeling it in fast. His thin pole was bent so much we were sure it would snap. The man put his own pole down and standing next to the boy, urged him to take it easy and reel in slowly until finally, they brought up a silver, palm-size fish. The man got the boy to calm down long enough to hold the line with the wiggling fish on the end, to take a photograph with a camera he pulled from a picnic basket. Then carefully, he unhooked it and let the boy throw it back in the water.

"That was a good fish. Two more like it would fill the frying pan," said the deckhand next to me.

The man and the boy caught a few more fish, some a bit bigger than the first one and, like the first, they had their picture taken and then threw them back in the water.

"Americans don't know anything about good eating," said a deckhand. "Over here, if you know how to boil water they call you *Chef.* You know what's the difference between their *Chefs* and an average cook? The *Chef* warms the food up after he takes out of the can."

Writing this now I can appreciate how far we had missed the point of that fishing incident.

One of the trips we took was to a small German town called Emden. It was during springtime and I remember going through a canal and seeing green meadows on both sides.

Another trip to Europe was to an oil terminal outside an English town named Carrington. There was a large green pasture near the place we docked, and the cook and the steward went out and picked dandelion greens. They were served later as a side dish to the pot roast we had for supper. They were very tasty and everyone thought it was nice of them to do it.

Our ship also made a trip to Marseille where we stayed one week and a trip to Copenhagen where we stayed a week unloading heating oil from Aruba. I don't remember much of our stay in the French port but of Copenhagen I remember Tivoli Gardens and the Little Mermaid statue and, for some strange reason, more vividly, a square in the middle of the city that I could get to by taking the public bus from the docks.

It was a large square with benches all around it, most of which were occupied by elderly locals sunning themselves. I managed to find an empty spot on a bench and spent some time people-watching. There were three food stands at the fringes of the square selling steamed sausage. A person sitting next to me got up and bought one and after noticing how he seemed to enjoy chewing on it when he sat back down, I decided to try one myself. The man put one between some bread and asked me something in his language which I didn't understand but I nodded and he must have interpreted as "yes" because he put relish and sauerkraut around it. I found out I liked it and I went back for another one. This time I pointed to the trays of condiments and in sign language which included a thumbs up gesture, I tried to tell him to put everything on. He cracked a smile and loaded as much as he could on it. I didn't want to return to the same bench—the man who gave me the idea to try it was still sitting there—so I sat on a bench on the opposite side of the square. After eating the second I still felt hungry but this time I went to a different food stand and had him load it with everything. I had never eaten any sausages of that kind, and I discovered I really liked them. By the time I took the bus to return to the ship I had eaten four fully loaded sausages, each time going to a different food stand and returning to a different bench.

I found out later, on a trip to New Haven, in Connecticut, that in America that kind of sausages are called "hot dogs."

(My earnest apologies for the let-down to those who went through the lines above, perhaps expecting to read about fierce storms in dark nights, with howling winds and ship-swallowing waves, or death-defying duels with blood thirsty pirates, only to read about dandelions being picked at an English countryside and about how I came to taste my first hot dog.)

*

On a trip to New Haven, Connecticut, during the winter, Antonis, the fireman of the twelve-to-four watch, took a tumble coming down the boiler room stairs during the shift change and had to be taken to the hospital. Drakos and the other fireman worked six-hour shifts till the replacement from Greece joined the ship in Aruba.

For a while, there was a lot of talk and speculation about whether Antonis took the fall on purpose, or if it was a real accident. "There are people who have made a profession out of slipping and falling down," said an old-timer. "I knew a man from Andros who every time the ship came to America, he would try to get hit by a city bus or by one of those yellow taxi cabs. Then he would go back to the island and live like a millionaire for a few months on the money he got from the American insurance."

"Only in this country," quipped another old-timer. "Anywhere else in the world all he would get would be a bag of pain pills and a ticket home, if that much."

(Later, when I was staying at the Rex Hotel between ships, I also met a man on his way back to Greece, who was bragging about the huge settlement he had gotten from the insurance after falling down the drydock of Bethlehem Steel in Hoboken.)

The company sent a new man in Aruba to replace Antonis and for a few days after his arrival he was the center of attention. Like any newcomer, he was the bearer of the latest developments on the island of Andros and of the whole country. This time the man was apologetic for the scant inventory of national news and local gossip. "I didn't get out of the house much," he said. "I was ashore only three weeks; usually it takes me longer than that where I can have a conversation with regular people without all the cuss words in my talk."

"It's the same thing with me," somebody else added. "It takes me a while to get used to life among regular people. And every time I put something on a shelf, like a bottle or a glass, I try to secure it as if the house was going to start rolling in a storm."

*

On the twenty-second of November 1963, I was in the engine room on my second twelve-to-four watch. We were transiting Lake Maracaibo on our way to La Salina to get a load of crude oil. Around two o'clock, not long after we had gone under the Maracaibo bridge, the engine cadet of the eight-to-twelve came running down the engine room and when he caught his breath, he said, "The radio operator just said that they shot John Kennedy, the president of America."

The rest of our day was spent speculating about who could have done it and why. Among the engine crew, it ended up being a tie between the Mafia and Castro, the way we saw it both sides had grudges against Kennedy.

*

During my sailing years, the Greek merchant marine was at its peak. Almost in every port, you could find a ship with a Greek crew.

All the seamen's bars had Greek records in their jukeboxes and anybody deriving an income from ships could parrot in Greek the necessary words to peddle their craft. The pimps could describe the age and physical attributes of their inventory and the taxi drivers their fare and their knowledge of places with the best entertainment. It seemed everyone thought that Greek was the language of the merchant mariners. I remember one time going ashore in Amuay Bay in Venezuela and hearing a taxi driver negotiating with a group of Norwegians standing next to us. It appeared the Norwegians had said his fare was too high because the taxi driver had answered back in Greek: *"Ohi pola lefta vre, ohi pola."* (Not much money man, not much.)

A few times, the *Andros Sea* delivered her cargo to Montreal, and we transited the Saint Lawrence Seaway. I remember admiring the greenery and the quaint houses on either side of the river. Near Quebec, the hotel Château De Frontenac stood on the riverbank like a castle out of a fairy tale. At the time I had no inkling or even imagined that many years later, on a vacation trip to the area with my wife and youngest daughter, I would spend three days in one of the suites at that place. (Funny how things work out in life.)

One time our ship unloaded cargo at the city of Elizabeth in New Jersey. While at the Maritime Academy, I had a pen pal from that city. She was in the eleventh grade of an American high school, and she had said she wanted to be a teacher. We had been corresponding for about a year but after I graduated from the academy, we hadn't exchanged any letters. I still remembered the girl's name and address, and a few times, when the ship was in an American port, I thought of looking up her phone number and calling her, but I always gave up at the last minute.

This time, while we were discharging in Elizabeth, I decided to ride the bus to Manhattan and during the ride I noticed we were passing my pen pal's street. I kept looking at the numbers on the houses and noticed that the bus made a stop in the block where her house was. I started to get off but by the time I reached the door, I changed my mind. I turned around and went back to my seat. Sometimes I wonder how that visit would have ended.

Another time we unloaded boiler fuel to one of the plants of Florida Power and Light Company in the port of West Palm Beach. Across the street from the port was a nightclub called Music Casters. On Saturday evening I and the fireman of my watch decided to take a look at the place. It was a much different nightclub than the ones we used to go to in other ports. It seemed to be frequented by young locals, most of them of high school age. The place was packed. We asked the person at the bar for a Seven-and-Seven, and they said they didn't serve alcohol, so we ordered a plain Coca-Cola. The music wasn't what we were familiar with, and the dancing, although interesting to watch the gyrating limber girls' bodies, was beyond our skills. We decided to conserve our vigor for Aruba, and after we finished our drinks, we went for a walk around the town.

Some years later, Brenda told me that she and her cousin, Cyrese, used to go there quite often, she was probably there the Saturday night we were there.

*

I found out that I could get the license for third engineer by taking the exam at the Liberian Consul's office, in New York. Then, if I were successful, I could get promoted by the company or get a job as an officer elsewhere. While the ship was unloading in Bayonne one time I went to The Consul's office in Manhattan and filled out the paperwork. I was told I had the choice of taking the test in English or in Greek. There was a small translation fee if I was to take it in Greek, but I thought it was worth it because I didn't feel confident about my English. The person at The Consulate gave me a list of the subjects I would be tested on, and I started studying every available minute.

Next time the *Andros Sea* went to New Jersey for dry docking at Bethlehem Steel in Hoboken, I volunteered to be the night engine-room watchman; that way, I could go to the Liberian Consul in Manhattan during the daytime and take the test. I used the quiet nighttime to study and prepare for the next day's test, and a few times, I dozed off. Once, the chief engineer, during his late-night rounds, shook me awake. “It’s not only *you* that will burn up if there’s a fire. The rest of us will burn along with you,” he said. He was a nice, understanding man, who tried to help anyone who would ask him.

Two days after I finished with the test, we left the shipyard heading for Venezuela to load. I thought I had done quite well in the exams and was looking forward to getting the third engineer’s license. I had studied all the subjects and had no difficulty writing my answers to any of the questions. Then one month later, when I visited the Liberian Consulate for the results, I received the shocking news; I had failed all subjects except math and drafting. Seeing my disbelief, the man at the consulate said I could review my test papers if I desired. I told him that I desired it, and when I looked at the translation, I lost all my politeness and shyness and started shouting at the clerk who had brought the papers.

“What kind of *bitsikomis* you hire?” I asked. Seeing he didn’t understand, I repeated: “What kind of bums, *beachcombers*, did you hire to do the translating? Did you check their credentials?”

I learned later that the American expression for what I did in front of the clerk, was *blow my top*. The man who did the translating had slaughtered my answers. His English must have been even worse than mine. The clerk spoke for a few minutes to a person in another office, then returned, and introduced him to me. “This is my boss,” he said. “He’s in charge of the licensing program.”

His boss was a nice man, a few years older than I, who gently, and patiently explained to me that there was the possibility the man who did the translation, a port engineer for the Onassis Company, might have done a bad job of it. “There is a process by which you may protest the results and have them re-evaluated,” he said. “That usually takes about three months and there are some fees involved. Judging from what I overheard, you seem to have a good understanding of the language. I would suggest you retake the exams, and this time take it in English.”

He told me where I could buy a copy of the Red Book, the book used for the American and the Liberian license exams and suggested I study it. Before leaving I told him that his office should be more careful about who they get to do the translating. "Who knows how many people he messed up the advancement of because he no knows enough good the language," I said. He smiled and said he would make a full report of the incident. Then he wished me luck on my test.

I hit the books, including the ship's instruction manuals, which were in English since the ship was built by Bethlehem Steel, and four months later, I was back at the licensing department of the Liberian Consul.

"Remember me?" I said to the nice young man in charge of the licensing program.

"Oh yes, Mr. Pitsios, the Rebel," he answered with a chuckle. I took the test again and this time I passed everything. One week later, on January seventeenth of 1964, I had my third engineer's diploma for *steam vessels of any horsepower*. I had it laminated at a print shop near the embassy and also had them laminate a smaller copy that I kept in my wallet.

At the time, Orion Shipping didn't have any third engineer's positions open, and I was too impatient to wait, so I turned in my resignation a few weeks after I got the license. I had been on board for fourteen months. She was a good ship, and she supplied me with many pleasant memories.

Before going back to Greece, I decided to spend some time in New York City. New York was where many of the main offices of major shipping companies were located and for someone like me who wanted to make a career in the marine shipping world, I considered familiarizing myself with their existence to be part of my basic training.

Again, I stayed at the Hotel Rex on Forty-Seventh Street and Broadway near Times Square, about a twenty-minute ride on the subway to Lower Manhattan, the hub of sea-borne transportation. The hotel was owned by a Greek family who must have had connections with the shipping companies because Greek seamen always stayed there on their way to or from their ships. Also, Greeks who were not seamen stayed there while waiting for the *SS Olympia*, the liner running between Piraeus and New York.

In a way, the hotel lobby served as the gathering place for New York Greeks. Some were meeting acquaintances on their way back home or just returning from there and others just hanging out. In the evenings, we would either watch American shows on the hotel's only television set or listen to those who lived in the area talk about their jobs: mostly painting bridges around the country or waitressing at the fancy restaurants like Copacabana in the winter, and the Catskills in the summer.

Other times we would swap sea stories or listen to the narration of a Greek visitor's odyssey of trying to find his cousin's house in Astoria or getting lost in the maze of subways. One of those seamen-in-transit that I remember was a seventy-year-old fireman who had just signed off a ship. He was tall and stout and on his way to Greece to attend his granddaughter's wedding. He was born in Constantinople (Istanbul) and had gone to sea at sixteen years of age as a coal stoker. He spoke five languages, had been to every port in the world, and could narrate stories about his life at sea during "the old days" in the most captivating way. When he was in the lobby, during the time he waited for the *Olympia* to arrive, the television never got turned on. We would goad him to get started and then sit around spellbound. One evening, an American relative of someone staying there attempted to turn the television on because the Jets were playing, and he almost got lynched.

Next to the hotel, in a long and narrow corridor-like area, was the minuscule luncheonette "Parthenon," run by Kostas, an immigrant from a mountain village in Greece. I used to eat breakfast there quite often: corn beef hash with two poached eggs on top or a three-egg feta-cheese omelet with three links of sausage, (no concerns about cholesterol those days). I usually sat at the counter across from the grill and watched him flip hamburgers and grilled cheese sandwiches. A cigarette was permanently dangling from the corner of his mouth, and sometimes its ashes would be added to the flavor. His talking was always about the same subject: his life in America and about his plans for the future. "As soon as I hit it big at the racetrack, I'll open up a classy place on the East Side and make a fortune. The *Mericani* (Americans) are gullible people you know; they'll eat anything you put in front of them."

Had I been able to see a few years into the future when I opened my own restaurant, I would have paid more attention to his cooking technique and asked questions about profit margins, portion sizes, and space utilization. Instead, I found out the hard way that the *Mericani* were neither gullible nor that they would eat anything one put in front of them, but I'm getting ahead of myself.

Three blocks from the hotel, near the Broadway theaters, were more Greek restaurants, all with larger dining rooms and larger menus than the Parthenon. My favorite was Molfetas' Restaurant. It reminded me of home. Their daily specials were kept on a hot table behind a glass wall, and I could point to the one I wanted. Since it was next to the theaters, the place must have been popular with actors because the walls were covered with signed photographs of stars that supposedly had eaten there

One block over from the restaurants, on Forty-Eighth and Broadway, was the Acropolis Cinema, which showed Greek movies. Directly across the street from the movie house, on the second floor of a commercial building, was the office of Mr. Pardalakis, the representative of the Greek Merchant Seamen's union in America. It was one large room, furnished with comfortable couches and chairs, and an American coffee pot that was always full.

Many Greek seamen when in New York spent time in his office, drinking coffee and catching up on the latest maritime gossip. Mr. Pardalakis, in his mid-fifties at the time, was always helpful and had a sincere interest in the welfare of the men. Besides refereeing disputes between seamen, captains and shipowners, he also helped in many other ways a seaman stranded in a foreign land might need help with, and never failed to offer paternal advice to young hotheads. Sometimes, shipping companies would call his office looking for available men to replace someone who jumped ship or got injured and had to stay in the hospital. Many people had gotten good-paying jobs through his office.

Most of those who knew him, when they signed off a ship, would always remember to bring him a small present from the foreign places they had been. Usually, the present was postage stamps of which he was an avid collector.

While trying to make up my mind whether I should go to Greece as a passenger on the *Olympia* or take a plane, I was occupying myself with the normal touristy things one does when in New York, like going to Radio City to see the Rockettes or watching the ice skaters at Rockefeller Plaza. In between, I would lounge in Mr. Pardalakis' office as a way of keeping my finger on the pulse of the maritime industry. One day a call came that kept Mr. Pardalakis talking on the phone for a while. When he hung up, he told the office audience that there were some cruise ships in Miami with an international crew, including some Greeks, in the engine room.

"Six months ago," he said, "I sent two engineers, a second and a third, down there and the owners seem to like them and are looking for more. This call right now, was for a third engineer on one of the ships called *Ariadne*. Any of you interested? They go on short cruises around the Caribbean."

I was the only engineer in his office at the time. "What kind of propulsion she's got?" I asked.

"It's steam turbines," said Mr. Pardalakis.

I thought for a moment, then I said, "I'll give it a try." It was a good opportunity to initiate my brand-new third engineer's license, and it would be an experience different from what I had known sailing with freighters and tankers up to now. My vacation in Greece could wait. The fact that it might upset the nice folks at the Greek Selective Service who were also waiting for me, didn't cross my mind.

Followed by an outpouring of good luck wishes, expressions of envy, and lots of advice on how to get a rich widow passenger to marry me, I left Mr. Pardalakis' office to catch a plane for Miami.

(That phone call, coupled with another one some years later, also from the same office, were "the forks on the road" in my life, but again, I am getting ahead of myself.)

CHAPTER EIGHT

The Cruise ship SS Ariadne

I reported onboard the *SS Ariadne* on January 20, 1964. Compared with today's cruise ships, she would be considered a miniature. Her total passenger capacity was about two hundred forty people, smaller than the janitorial staff in some of the behemoths of today.

She sailed out of Miami, and a few times out of Fort Lauderdale, for trips around the Caribbean islands: Bahamas, Jamaica, St. Lucia, Haiti, and, occasionally, venturing as far as Bermuda. The first, second, and third engineers, and the second electrician were Greeks. The chief electrician was German, and the firemen and oilers were from parts of the Caribbean—mostly from Jamaica and Honduras.

All officers were required to wear uniforms—khakis for work and whites off hours. We were also strongly encouraged to dine with the passengers in the main dining room. Each officer was assigned to a table in the dining room, and we could, if we wanted, dine there every night. The only one from the engine crew who did that was the German chief engineer and, on some occasions, the first engineer, John Dourambeis, and the chief electrician.

When we were not working, we could go to the lounge and the nightclub and dance with the passengers. Quite a few officers on that ship developed acquaintances that went beyond the postcard-exchange stage.

Usually, once a week the ship would call into Nassau in the Bahamas, and sometimes to Freeport in Grand Bahama. I knew the port of Freeport before it became a port. When I was on the tanker *Andros Sea*, we unloaded Bunker C at a bunkering station there. That's where I had spent my first Christmas at a tropical place. At that time, they had just started to turn the area into a resort, and the only non-locals there were the construction workers building roads, dredging the harbor, and constructing hotels. By the time the *Ariadne* started visiting, a few vacation homes had been completed, and a couple of hotels with casinos were in operation.

Almost twice a month, the ship would visit the island of Jamaica. We would go to Montego Bay, Ocho Rios, and Port Antonio, the place where the famous actor Errol Flynn had a vacation home. In Ocho Rios, the main attraction was Dunn's River Falls. The water comes from a spring farther inland and flows into the sea through a series of small falls, where tourists can slide and splash like children in a water park. We also went to Kingston, where passengers could take glass-bottom boat rides and see the old Port Royal. For the night tours, the cruise director had to call for police escorts because, apparently, there were lots of descendants from the pirate days.

On one of the trips to Kingston, my old ship, the *Andros Sea,* happened to be in port, and I had a nice get-together with some of the old shipmates. The old chief engineer, the one who was onboard when I was taking my examinations while the ship was in dry dock, was still there. He said he was glad I put my license to good use, but when I invited some of the men to come and visit me, he said they didn't have time. I think he didn't want any more of his men getting ideas.

*

We made a few trips to Port-au-Prince, where I saw firsthand what bad government can do to a place. Haiti was the first colony in this hemisphere to gain independence, yet at the time, it was one of the poorest and most disorganized nations in the world, thanks to a series of bad leaders from Henri Christophe to Papa Doc Duvalier, the one on the throne when we visited.

Some of the engine crew of SS Ariane, 1965
Dimitrios, the electrician, me, Chief Engineer Heron Stamelos, First Assistant Giannis Dourambeis, and 3rd engineer Michael

I remember when the purser first said we were going to Port-au-Prince; I was thrilled because I found the islands of the French colonies more interesting. A few months earlier, we visited Martinique and Guadeloupe and had pleasant experiences.

That first time in Haiti, I, Dimitris, the Greek electrician, and two others embarked for our trip ashore late in the afternoon. The chief mate had said the locals preferred American dollars to their own *gourdes*, so we didn't bother changing any. While walking towards a group of taxis parked beneath a row of palm trees, Dimitris kept flipping a set of metallic worry beads and humming the lines of a Greek song praising the sexiness of Creole women. We told the first taxi driver who came forward to meet us to take us to Citadel Henri

Cristophe. "Okie Talkie," he said. "Five dollar. You pay first, five dollar. Need gasoline."

I started to count my part, but Dimitris stopped me. "Hell no," he shouted, "that's how we got screwed in Kingston; the man took our money and disappeared. We are not paying you till you get us there," he told the driver. The driver, a short, skinny, nervous type, with a slight limp, mumbled something in Haitian, then said, "Okie Talkie" and everybody piled in.

The taxi was an old Chevrolet, hand-painted in high-gloss purple, orange, and yellow, with alternating wavy stripes. Inside, the dashboard was decorated with three, equally spaced, palm-size, oval photographs of Brigitte Bardot, Marilyn Monroe, and Elizabeth Taylor; all in wet bathing suits. Between, and around the photographs, plastic beads of the same outside colors were glued in wavy rows, and a gold-colored plastic crucifix dangled from the mirror.

We drove on a bumpy road, through neighborhoods with cinderblock, one-room houses, tin shacks, and hordes of barefooted children kicking semi-deflated balls. "This doesn't look anything like Martinique," said Dimitris. "Haven't seen any trees or any flowers anywhere. If somebody asks me about it, I'll tell them Port-au-Prince is a poor, trashy place, overpopulated with stray dogs and destitute people."

About three kilometers from our start, a few meters short of reaching the top of a hill, the old Chevrolet started coughing and sputtering and finally died out completely. To the left side of the road stood a big, rich-looking house, with tall, Greek-style white columns in the front and rows of windows on all three floors. On either side of the front entrance were guard posts, with a huge Haitian in each, armed with long rifles, pistols on both hip-sides, and bandoliers crisscrossing their chest. Our taxi had conked out almost in front of their door.

At first, the driver turned and faced us and, sounding as if it was our fault, said, "No gasoline, *pas d'essence, petrol, pas.*" Then he looked outside, saw where he'd stopped, and jumped out and started pushing at the car and shouting in Haitian, his words ringing with the desperation of a drowning man. Almost in an instant, the guards were out of their sentry boxes, yelling and firing their rifles in the air.

"Let's get out and push this jalopy before they start aiming lower," I said, and all of us scrambled out and joined the driver. Three leaned on the back, and I was on the opposite side of the driver, all of us straining to get the old car rolling. It was slow going. The car was too heavy and the hill too steep, and we were barely moving. A few minutes later, six more guards ran out, grabbed everybody as they were being pushed, and dragged them towards the building. Just then, the old Chevrolet started rolling back, turned slightly right, and took aim at the front door. The driver yelled something, broke loose from the group, and dashed towards the car. Everybody else sprang out of the way, taking cover behind the columns and the sentry boxes. The guards kept shouting to the driver, and he kept shouting back, while frantically pulling on the emergency brake. Finally, after lots of stomping and pulling, he managed to stop the obstinate old Chevy, just millimeters from the fancy crystal coat-of-arms of the front door. Everybody stared in silence at the back of the car for a while till the guards started shouting and pointing at it with their rifles.

"I guess they want us to get this damn thing back to where it came from," I said, and we started pushing.

"If we had paid the damn dollar, we wouldn't be in this fix," gasped one of the men.

When the car was back on the road, the driver took a gas can from the trunk, said something about *petrol,* and asked us for some money. We gave him five dollars, and he signaled for us to wait there, then took off, presumably in search of a gas station.

By the time he came back, about an hour later, the Haitian guards had cleaned us of all our cigarettes and had started serious negotiations for our wristwatches. The ordeal had killed our desire for sightseeing, and we told the driver to take us back to the ship.

During lunch the next day, Dimitris told those in the officers' dining room about our little adventure. "Now I see what makes these people desperate enough to get in washtubs and try to get the hell out of here," he concluded. "This country is run by a bunch of thieves with guns."

"You're too naïve, my friend," Dourambeis cut in from across the table. "It's a conspiracy; the big powers, the Americans and the French, like to keep it that way; it suits their purpose." For an instant, I thought I was seeing one of the coffee-house regulars in my village. They, too, when they sat under the plane tree in the square, armed with a heavy set of amber worry-beads and occupying three chairs each, professed to see through the most intricate international conspiracies and have an explanation for the most baffling of diplomatic maneuvers.

*

On the *Ariadne* most of the passengers were of the senior citizen category, with an occasional granddaughter dragged along. One time, the chief purser announced that for the next cruise, the ship was fully booked by a girls' college. Many of us got our hopes up and made sure we were stocked up on aftershave lotions and that our dancing shoes were polished. Then, when the passengers started boarding in Miami, we, freshly shaved and hair greased, leaned over the rails waiting for the college beauties to come up the gangway.

They did come up all right, slowly and feebly, in wheelchairs and walkers, and supporting each other. The purser, a Spaniard, with a typically Mediterranean sense of humor, conveniently had left out the part that the girls' college had booked the cruise for a class reunion of some ancient year.

There were also three other passenger ships sailing out of Miami during that time: the *Yarmouth Castle*, the *Bahama Star*, and the *Florida*. Most of the engineers on them were also Greeks, and I got to know them well. George Vazeos, the chief engineer for *Yarmouth Castle,* was close friends with our first assistant engineer, and since our ships had almost the same schedule, we saw a lot of him when he visited our ship.

Vazeos was short, round, bald, and in his early sixties, making him the oldest in both age and appearance among our group. Maybe that's why he considered it his responsibility to give advice, whether he was asked or not, on how the rest of us should live our lives. He seemed to be proud of what *he* had accomplished in his own life: He had left the island of Hios and gone to sea when he was fifteen years old. His first job on ships was shoveling coal, then advanced to the engineering ranks when the government, in times of extreme need of manpower during war, issued licenses to those with sufficient shipboard service. Like many old-timers who got their license through experience, he harbored mistrust and skepticism toward young license holders who were graduates of maritime academies.

When in port, Vazeos almost never went ashore. He would either be visiting our ship or, according to those who knew him, going over his bank statements in his cabin and watching the exchange rate of the dollar with the drachma. He kept saying he would soon retire to his island and live like a pasha on the money he had accumulated through the clever handling of his affairs. His motto was, "You got to know how to handle your craft to sell it high." All the engineers on the four cruise ships knew he didn't like to exert himself. We were all familiar with the tricks he used to show the underlings his knowledge and to appear indispensable to the higher-ups in the company. Sometimes, especially when a superintendent from the main office was visiting, he would create a problem in the engine room and, after everyone else gave up, he would fix it in the presence of the office person. (Some years later, his tendency not to exert himself was to play a pivotal role in shaping the rest of my life.)

To those who expect to read about exciting and scandalous adventures from my time on the *Ariadne*, I'm afraid they will be disappointed. Nothing titillating or of a scandalous nature comes to mind as I struggle to fill the page with something worthy of the memoir-writing expectations. The only event we thought came close to that at the time was when the second electrician, a handsome young man in his early twenties from a small village in Greece, was convinced by a fifty-year-old divorcée from California to follow her in San Francisco as her boyfriend. The cruise director said he would be her "toy boy."

At the time, we also thought it was funny, although it was anything but that, when an older lady from a cabin on C deck stepped out on the passageway calling, "Help, we're sinking." She had seen water coming out of her toilet when the sewage pump switch failed to start, and the holding tank overflowed. (Sewage treatment plants had not been made mandatory on passenger ships yet. It was not unusual to see things that go through the ship's toilets float in the water of a harbor.)

From the crew of the *Ariadne*, two people stand out in my memory: John Dourambeis, the first assistant engineer, and Petros, the wine steward. I thought both must have been disciples of George Vazeos because they had similar ideas as to how to highlight the importance of what they were doing.

Petros used to sail as a deck officer on the rust-buckets trading between the United States and Cuba in the pre-Castro era. His favorite story, which he narrated whenever he had an audience, was how he earned his promotion from third mate to chief mate. "The ship on which I was third mate," his story went, "used to call on Cienfuegos once a month. Sometimes we would anchor outside the port and wait for a berth to become available. There was a spot in the bay, the remnants of an old volcano crater, where if you dropped an anchor there, you would lose it for sure; it was over a thousand feet deep. I was good friends with the local pilot, and he showed me where that spot was, and I remembered it. On one of the trips, the ship's owner happened to be sailing with us. When we approached Cienfuegos, we were told we would have to anchor and go in the next day. The owner was on the bridge at the time, and the captain, wanting to show off, decided not to wait for the pilot to take us to anchorage. I was on watch, but I didn't tell anybody about the crater. Instead, I stood by the bridge-wing keeping an eye on the markers ashore. When I heard the captain order the starboard anchor to be dropped, I ran in the bridge yelling, 'No, no, no.' I grabbed the bullhorn and told the bosun at the windlass to hold off. 'You've got to have the bow lined up with the lighthouse and have the cathedral dome about thirty degrees to your starboard to clear the caldera,' I told the captain. 'You'll lose the anchor if you drop it now.' The owner stood next to him. The next day, as soon as we docked, he went to the pilot's office, and when he came back, he told the captain to pack up. The chief mate got his job, and I got the chief's."

I don't know whether there is a caldera outside Cienfuegos harbor, or whether that incident really happened, but during the time I knew him as a wine steward on the *Ariadne*, I had plenty of proof of his scheming. When working, he used to pace the dining room dressed in the regalia of a true Middle Ages sommelier, with the gold tasting cup and the key to the wine cellar dangling from his neck on golden chains and the white towel folded over his left arm. If someone had left an unfinished bottle of wine on his table, he would save it, and when he saw a person who had the potential of a good tipper, he would approach them and ask if they would accept a glass of wine from him. That almost always brought a good tip. Another one of his tip-extracting tricks was the souvenirs he gave. He would take a carton of cigarettes ashore in Port-au-Prince, (we could buy a carton from the ship's steward for a dollar back then), and exchange one pack for one miniature native painting with the local artists. Then, a day before the end of the cruise, he would offer them as souvenirs to the good-tipper prospects. Most of them were thrilled; some would even ask him to write a dedication in the back.

In those days, tips were not included in the cruise ticket. The waiters used to bribe the purser to get the birthdates of passengers whose birthdays fell during the cruise, so they could present them with a small cake with a sparkler at their table. (Nowadays, the purser and the cruise line would probably be sued for invasion of privacy.)

Our first assistant, John Dourambeis, was in his forties, medium height, roundish, with puffy cheeks, and a flexible, beachball-sized stomach. He had the talent of making even the most ordinary occurrence seem like a Hollywood thriller, and the simplest of his job tasks a space-age achievement. "He can make putting new packing in the bilge pump seem like rocket science," one of the third engineers had said one time.

I'm sure the people at the company office were convinced the *Ariadne* couldn't run without John's seal of approval on anything that had to do with their ship. When, one time, the chief steward complained to the main office that some of the meat had gone bad due to insufficient refrigeration, John countered that the meat was spoiled when it was received and should not have been accepted. He was so convincing that the company decreed that from then on, an engine department representative should be present when the steward's provisions were brought on board, to verify their quality.

He was one of the few officers from the engine department who utilized the privilege of dining with the passengers. Then later, he would narrate to the rest of us how he thrilled everyone at his table with his super-embellished adventures on the high seas and in ports in exotic corners of the globe. "The little lady from Oklahoma almost fainted when I told the story about the time I was with a freighter, loaded with coconut shells from the Philippines heading to Rotterdam, and got caught in a typhoon, and the pipe supplying the steam to the ship's steering mechanism broke and we were rudderless for six hours just a mile from the widow-making cliffs of Luzon."

John was quick to point out that, out of concern for the passengers' peace of mind, his stories about challenging storms and treacherous reefs always happened in faraway places, way beyond the cruising range of our good ship *Ariadne*.

Although John's handling of the English language would make a teacher cringe, he didn't let that detail hinder the narration of his story. If he didn't know how to say something, he filled in the void with body movements and facial expressions. When he was telling a story, every part of his body participated in the telling: his arms, his face, his dimples, and his flexible stomach, all got involved in the performance, to the delight of the audience.

For us, his colleagues, John had a different inventory of stories. One of his favorites was the intentional grounding of the ship he was on some years before joining the *Ariadne*. "That was back in 1959. I was third engineer on a five-thousand toner floating rust-blister," he would start. "Everything was wrong with her. And, on top of it, the owner owed a fortune to every bank in the world. He worked out a scheme with the captain and the chief engineer, and they found a reef a few hours outside Jamaica that, supposedly, wasn't shown in the charts the ship had onboard. In the middle of the night, while we were on our way to Port Antonio to load sugar, they ran full speed on top of that reef. We got picked up by a Norwegian freighter later that day and taken to Kingston. The owner met us at the dock and put us up in a super-fancy hotel. He got all of us together and gave us a big speech about how sorry he was about us having to go through the accident, and he'd make sure we got our full pay and one month's extra salary on top for our hardship as soon as he got the money from the insurance. 'When the insurance people ask you about the accident,' he said, 'just tell them the truth and it'll be over soon. All of you will get your money and will go home.'

Well, the insurance hearing lasted two weeks, and in the meantime, we were sleeping at that fancy hotel and eating fancy food at the restaurant. For the first week, the waiter who stood next to my table would pull my plate away before I finished it. I used to be hungry the rest of the day until somebody told me that in the fancy English tables, when you put your knife and fork on your plate a certain way, it means you're done eating, and if you put them another, it means you want more."

"I bet you made up for it after you learn what the *other* way was," somebody always cut in. "Did you get the extra month pay?"

"No, never did. The insurance found out the grounding was on purpose and refused to pay."

"How did they find out?"

"It turns out, the owner had told the captain, the chief engineer, and the chief mate to say that the hydraulic hose to the steering gear busted and couldn't steer, but seeing they were in deep water, they didn't bother to lower an anchor. He never bothered to tell the cook what to say, and when the insurance man asked him where he was during the grounding, he said he was in the kitchen cleaning the grill after cooking steaks."

"'Do you usually cook steaks in the middle of the night?' the insurance man asked him.

"'No,' the cook said. 'This was the first time, and I thought it was strange, but they said it was the captain's birthday, and they were having a party.'

"'Did you notice anything else strange?' the man asked.

"'Well… when I went to pick up the plates afterwards, they told me not to bother, and they started throwing them overboard. They watched them skip on top of the waves and laughed. They gave me a bottle of wine and sent me back.'"

At this point, John always paused to allow us to digest the meaning of the story. Then, just to be sure there was no misinterpretation, he would conclude. "You see, the captain felt sorry for the cook who would be doing futile work washing the plates, but they didn't think to take him into their scheme. That, and after checking with the captain's passport that showed a birthday three months away, lost the case for them."

*

When the German chief engineer of the *Ariadne* left to go on vacation, the company replaced him with a Greek man named Heron Stamelos. He came from an upper-class family in Athens and was a sociable and well-educated fellow. In the evenings, most of us, the Greek officers, would gather in his cabin for drinks and conversation. He was well-read, and he liked to keep up with what was happening in the world. In those gatherings, politics, and American politics in particular, was the main subject of discussion.

When we docked in Miami, almost always, two Greek seamen would come on board and have lunch and dinner with us. Then, when leaving, they usually took some more food with them and smuggled a few packs of cigarettes. I was told they had worked on a Greek tanker and, while unloading in Miami, a fuel line ruptured, and they got burned badly. (They always wore long-sleeved shirts, buttoned all the way up.)

"They've filed a lawsuit," Stamelos had said, "but the shipping company lawyers keep postponing the hearing of their case, hoping they'll run out of money, give up, and go home. If their case is heard in Greece, they'll get pennies."

All of us were sympathetic toward the two burned comrades. Although the American prestige, as seen by outsiders, was waning at the time due to the Cuba fiasco and the Vietnam uncertainty, we, who had closer contact with the country and were familiar with how things worked, knew that, despite the recent blunders, if anyone was looking for justice, the place to find it was in America.

*

Those longing to travel, when hearing the names of the places we visited, Barbados, Bahamas, Bermuda, Jamaica, Martinique, Guadeloupe, and so on, they were becoming *green with envy*, as the Americans say. "You're getting paid to be on vacation," some would say, and I could see in their eyes that they wished they could swap places with me. But the novelty had worn off for me after a few months, and it was becoming boring. It was the same ports, the same sights, the same entertainment, even the passengers we carried started to seem the same to me.

In Nassau, there was an Honorary Greek Counselor, and during one of the ship's visits there, I went to his office and applied for a Greek passport. The Counselor was a commercial fisherman by trade, who owned a small fleet of fishing boats, and, I guess, he went after the Counselor's post for the prestige of the office. I found him sitting behind a battered desk at the far wall, under a portrait of King Paul and Queen Frederica. After weaving my way through stacks of lobster traps and mounds of fishing net to get to him and I told him what I wanted. He wrote the information on a piece of gray fish-wrapping paper and told me he would have it in two weeks.

When my passport arrived, I went a few blocks over to the American Embassy and had a tourist visa stamped on it. From then on,

I planned to use that visa when I signed off a ship to stay extra time and do sightseeing in America.

When I told George Vazeos that I was signing off, he thought I was crazy. "Where are you going to find it better than this?" he said. "It breaks my heart to see young people lacking the common sense to see it when God is handing them the good life on a silver platter. You're going to be galivanting all over creation, squandering your money and your youth. Didn't they teach you anything about life at that fancy school your parents sent you?"

"Well," I said, "everybody here seems to be satisfied with my work, I can always come back when I'm through with my *gallivanting*, as you call it."

Before I got off the ship, he gave me a large envelope full of stamps he had been collecting and told me to give it to Mr. Pardalakis, the seamen's union representative, in New York, with his regards.

The chief engineer, Heron Stamelos, also signed off at the same time, and I traveled with him to New York. He had seen in the *Miami Herald* an advertisement for someone wanting his car to be driven there, and he arranged to take it. Back then, there were agencies that would find licensed drivers to deliver the cars of those who didn't want to drive them themselves to where they were going. For us, it was an inexpensive way of getting to New York while seeing some of the country. That drive northward was my first glimpse at parts of America other than the commercial waterfront places I used to visit with the ships. I marveled at the thick forests, the wide-open spaces where nobody seemed to live. Some of the farms we were passing, were so huge that the tractor at the far end of it could be seen as no bigger than a grasshopper.

We had left Miami on a bright, sunny January day in short-sleeved shirts, then as we kept getting closer to our destination, we started pulling sweaters and overcoats out of the suitcases. By the time we got to New York three days later, the snow was about 12 inches deep, and we wore overcoats.

*

While in New York, I took the examinations for the second engineer's license. This time, I decided to go for the combined *steam-and-motor* ticket. It appeared that, despite the old-timer's predictions that the diesel-engine type of propulsion would fizzle out and be forgotten in a few years, it kept getting more and more popular.

Someone at the Rex Hotel where I was staying said he enrolled in an adult education class teaching English to those whose English was not their mother language. That particular someone was boasting that he was dating a hot Jewish woman he met in that class. "She was driving a tank for two years in the Israeli army," he said.

My time onboard the *Ariadne,* where I frequently had to communicate with people who did not speak Greek, convinced me that my English-speaking skills needed a lot of improvement. That, and the possibility that I may also be lucky and have a hot woman as a classmate did some additional convincing, and I signed up for the next session.

There was indeed a diverse and interesting group of people in my class coming from different parts of the world. Some of them provided the inspiration for characters in my book *Walking in the Light,* when Kostas, the main character, decides to take English lessons.

Stamelos was hired as a port engineer with a well-paying American shipping company that was operating six tankers with Liberian flags and asked me to go on one of them as a third engineer. It was three weeks after I started the English class and I hated to drop out, but the salary they offered was too good to pass up.

At the time, the ship was unloading in New Haven, Connecticut, and, since Stamelos had to go on board, we went together. The ship's name was *Coral Trader*, an old ship with a Burmeister diesel engine, that it was everything the old-timers used to tell me about. She was leaking oil and exhaust gases from every connection, was clankingly noisy, and we spent all the time in port changing pistons and cleaning turbochargers. The first assistant engineer was working almost twenty-four hours a day trying to keep that engine running.

It was the first ship I had been on with that type of propulsion, and that old rust bucket made a big contribution to my education of large diesel engines. We were constantly working on that engine: changing, inspecting, cleaning, reconditioning, and replacing every component. Although I hated it at the time, I had to admit I learned a lot.

And, thanks to the ship's chief engineer, I also learned a lot about people. The chief was short and round with shifty eyes and appeared to be in his mid-fifties. During the time at sea, he would be in his cabin or in the officers' lounge in his crisp khakis, drinking coffee. Then, when we picked up the pilot to enter port, he would put on a pair of gray coveralls that hadn't been washed since he signed on and spread a stack of blueprints on his desk. When someone from headquarters walked into his office, they found a man looking like he had been up all night poring over a mind-boggling collection of pipe drawings and instruction manuals. There had been a problem with the auxiliary boiler fuel line, the chief would explain, and he had been up all night to get it fixed so the ship could discharge the cargo on time. Every trip was a different hypothetical problem, which he always managed to solve just in the nick of time. The pencil pushers of the main office thought he was the most loyal employee and patted each other on the back for having discovered him.

During my sailing days, it was a common belief among a ship's crews that the one who knew somebody in the administrative office, even if it was the janitor, was having connections with the company. He was called a *company man* and, whether intentionally or not, in many cases, went around with a chip on his shoulder. I guess, because of the friendship I had developed with Stamelos, and because he had introduced me to some of the company office staff, his secretary, a lady in her fifties, and an *expeditor*, a university student who was running errands, I, too, was perceived to be a *company man*. Quite possibly, the chief engineer on the *Coral Trader*, when he saw Stamelos and me having an informal conversation on the dock while the ship was tying up, assumed I was an embedded office spy, and he couldn't pass up the opportunity to make me look bad.

The fiasco with the main engine cooling water cut-off valve was probably his idea of making me look bad in the eyes of the rest of the crew. It was on the second voyage, on the way to Maracaibo, when the chief told me to open that valve for inspection. "I suspect it doesn't open all the way," he said. "I ordered new parts for it in case we need to replace something; they're in a box next to the valve. You'll need to work fast because we have to stop the engine and we'll be adrift."

Normally, that was a task for the first assistant engineer, but the chief said he was in bed, sick. I had the eight-to-twelve watch and I would do the repair on overtime, after my watch. At exactly one o'clock, I notified the bridge and the engine-room watch, and as soon as they stopped the engine, my helper and I started taking the valve apart. Ten minutes after I started, and every ten minutes after that, I kept being bombarded by calls from the bridge: "Are you about finished? How much longer? Hurry it up, we're in a high-traffic area."

I took the valve apart and immediately found the problem; it was a gate valve, and the gate had broken and stuck partially closed. I got the replacement part and got ready to put it together. I had told the bridge messenger the repair would take about an hour, but as it turned out, it had taken me that long to get the valve open. Almost all the bolts were corroded and had to be chiseled loose. Then, when I got the new gate from the box and tried to put it together, I discovered that the stem wouldn't screw into it. I spent some time cleaning the threads, thinking they may be damaged, and at the same time, I kept answering the bridge that I would be through in twenty minutes.

"That's what you said half an hour ago," was the third mate's answer. I tried assembling it again and again, and every time I got the same result: it wouldn't fit. I was way past the original hour and all the twenty-minute extensions I had told the bridge, and I was desperately trying to get the damn thing done.

Soon after, the chief engineer, who all this time had been drinking coffee in the officer's lounge, came over. "We've been drifting for over an hour, let me see what's got you stumped over here," he said and picked up the two valve pieces I was trying to assemble. He glanced at them and put them back down almost immediately. "Can't you tell these don't match? They're threaded differently; one is right-handed and the other left. You got the wrong part."

"It was clearly marked for this valve," I said. "It was the only one in the box."

"Makes no difference where it was, it's still the wrong part. I thought you were an engineer." He turned to my helper and spoke directly to him as if he didn't consider me capable of doing even the closing. "Go ahead and close the damn valve before we end up on the rocks." Seeing the helper's puzzled look, he added: "Yes, close it without the gate; it'll be always open."

The helper and I finished the job in silence, put up the tools, and I went to my cabin. I was stunned. Feelings of incompetence and uselessness brought on by the memories of the spilled oil in Singapore and, from even farther back, of the time the goat I was supposed to be watching ate the fig graft of my father's favorite tree near the farmhouse. The chief's words hurt as much as my father's scolding.

It was careless of me not to check the threads when I first saw that the parts didn't fit. Yes, it had taken much longer to dismantle the valve, and yes, the bridge was calling every ten minutes, which was making me nervous, but those were excuses. The chief engineer had probably told the first assistant to stay away on purpose, so he could see how I would handle the job.

After that, a feeling that everyone was smirking behind my back when I was walking by got lodged permanently in my head, and I turned in my resignation. The captain tried to talk me out of it, but I had made up my mind. I signed off in Maracaibo on the thirteenth of July 1965. I had been on board for two-and-a-half months.

As I write this, it becomes obvious that I had mishandled the whole *Coral Trader* affair. Had I been more thoughtful, I could have used the situation to my advantage. After all, it was the chief engineer's and the first assistant's responsibility to check the correctness of the parts before accepting them from the supplier. There was even the possibility that he might have known the part was wrong, but at that time, I hadn't heard the American saying, "The best defense is a good offense."

The ship's agent booked me on a flight from Maracaibo to Caracas on a Venezuelan airline, and from there I was to get on a Pan American plane to New York. The flight to Caracas made an intermediate stop at the small town of Maiquetía. While looking out of the window during the approach, I noticed that Maiquetía was a resort town with long white beaches; not a bad place for a stressed young merchant seaman to unwind. I changed my ticket and stayed three days at a seaside hotel. I spent most of my time on long walks, lying on the beach, and watching Bonanza on television in the hotel lobby. (The show was dubbed in Spanish, and I thought Hoss Cartwright sounded hilarious speaking that language.)

When I was back in New York, I camped at the Hotel Rex and tried to put the *Coral Trader* out of my mind. I took a block of Venezuelan postage stamps to Pardalakis for his collection and resumed playing tourist.

This time I did some *real* tourist things: I spent a whole day visiting the Statue of Liberty and made two trips to Flushing Meadows to see the World's Fair.

CHAPTER NINE

When my bank balance signaled that my playing-tourist time was coming to an end, I decided to try shipping out with National Bulk Carriers—known as NBC among seafarers. Among people in our kind of work, they had the reputation of being one of the best-paying companies. One day, two other seamen and I took the subway from the Hotel Rex to their office on Rector Street, in Lower Manhattan, to apply for jobs. Before going up to the twenty-second floor for the interview, we stood in the lobby, near the elevators, rehearsing what we would say to the personnel man. The idea was to throw all the necessary information at him from the very beginning, which we thought would keep him from asking questions and would let him know our English was less than perfect.

In the middle of our rehearsal, a distinguished-looking man, about thirty, stepped out of the elevator, and when he heard us speaking Greek, he paused and introduced himself. He said his name was Captain Petros Katsaros. He was a bit taller than I was, with brown eyes and black hair combed like Tony Curtis, the movie star. He wore a gray suit and tie and carried a briefcase, which made me think he was a bigwig at the company.

We told him why we were there, and he said he had recently signed off from one of their ore carriers. We asked him what kind of person was the man who was doing the hiring, and what kinds of questions he'd be asking.

"He wants to know how much experience you have with their types of ships and if your English is good enough to communicate with the others," he said.

I asked him what he sailed as, and that seemed to have touched a sensitive nerve. He lit a cigarette and took a deep drag before answering. "I've been sailing for them as chief mate for three years, and of that, almost half a year with a master's diploma. The goofy old codgers up there," he nodded toward the top of the building, "keep telling me they don't have a captain's position open." He took another deep puff on his cigarette. "The man at the license bureau said I scored the highest he'd seen in years, but that wimp pencil-pusher up there tells me, 'no position open yet.'" The last four words were in a squeaky voice, presumably mimicking the wimpy person *up there*.

"They called me to come and talk to them today, and I thought it was about the captain's job on the *Bulker Express*, my old ship. Her captain is a sickly old walrus that should have retired years ago. Instead, they asked me to go back as chief mate again, 'to help the old man out,' they said." He took a deep puff on his cigarette and then blew out the smoke with the force of a turbine exhaust. "I told them, 'The old man has one foot in the grave. I'll be doing two jobs: mine and his.' They said it would be good training experience for me. I said I've had plenty of training experience, and I've been ready to be captain for a long time. I told them 'Goodbye' and walked out." He ground his cigarette in the ashtray with vengeance. "What's the use of having a captain's diploma if I can't use it?"

With the tutoring of Captain Petros, we rehearsed the anticipated conversation until one of us got enough nerve to push the button to the twenty-second floor. As we stepped into the elevator, one of the guys crossed himself. Petros saw it and grinned. "Good luck but remember: Heaven has a weird sense of humor."

We told the receptionist we were there for the three o'clock interview with "Mister Personnel." She ushered us into an adjacent office and said we would be called in shortly. About thirty minutes later, she said we could go in now. "One at a time," she clarified when all three of us jumped up.

The other two pushed me ahead, and I stepped into a wood-paneled office that smelled of cigar smoke. I said good afternoon to the heavy-set man behind the desk and, almost in the same breath, told him my name, that I was a licensed second engineer for steam and motor vessels of unlimited horsepower, that I was a hard worker, that I thought very highly of the National Bulk Carriers Company, and that I would be proud to become a permanent member of the company.

The personnel man listened to my speech with a hint of a smile while scribbling something on a notepad. When I finished, he spoke slowly and clearly, mixing his talk with a few Greek words, as if to show that my monologue, delivered at machine-gun speed, had not fooled him. He did offer me a position as a third engineer on one of their ships. If I perform well, he said, I could be promoted in a few months.

The Tanker Mustang Island, 1965

At that time, demand for merchant marine officers was high. It was not uncommon to see officers sailing in positions one rank above their license. Men with third engineer's license sailed as Seconds, and second engineers sailed as first assistants. But it seemed that NBC, since its pay scale was much higher than everyone else's and its food famously abundant, was not in urgent need of people.

I didn't want to gamble on how long it would be until I got promoted. It meant trusting others who could or couldn't report that I was "performing well." I told the personnel man I would think about it and let him know soon.

The next day, Pardalakis, who also moonlighted for many of us as our mail-forwarding address, got me a job as first assistant engineer on *Mustang Island.*

"She's an old Navy supply tanker, with Liberian flag," he said. "She's American-built, which means she's a comfortable ship, and the owners are Americans out of Texas, which means you'll be getting plenty of overtime. Right now, she's down in Baltimore getting a complete overhaul; they expect to sail in a couple of weeks. The port engineer is a Greek fellow. He's got the rest of the crew taken care of, but he needs a first assistant, and since you got your second's license, I can send you with no problem." He paused and searched through a stack of papers. "Ah, here's the address." He copied it and handed it to me. "I sent them a captain earlier this morning; he's probably there by now." A couple of old timers reading one-year-old Greek magazines wished me good luck and said I was very lucky to get the first's job so young. (I was twenty-three at the time.)

I took the Greyhound bus to Baltimore and reported to the chief engineer the next morning. It was the end of August 1965.

The chief engineer of *Mustang Island* was an elderly Greek man who lived in Uruguay. He told me he was already drawing a pension but took this job to pay for a farm he was buying outside Montevideo. "You'll have a free hand in running the engine room. I'll concentrate on doing the paperwork," he said. "The port engineer told me the owners expect detailed reports from the captain and me every month." He took a sip of whiskey and, gesturing with his glass-holding hand toward the bottle, asked me if I wanted a drink. I said I might get one later after I got signed on and headed for the captain's office.

On the way midship, I stopped on the catwalk and examined the two large piles of scrap in the middle of the deck. They consisted of old pipes and cut-up pieces of rusty steel plate. Next to those piles were about a dozen fifty-five-gallon drums full of thick rust flakes that must have come from the deck and the cargo tank bulkheads. Looking at all that obsolescence made me wonder what shape the engine-room machinery was in. *It'll be a challenge running her,* I thought.

I knocked on the captain's door, and I heard a voice I thought sounded familiar say, "Come on in."

I went in, and after a moment of slight shock, I said, "Good morning, Captain Petro."

"Oh, hi there," he answered, just as surprised. "The shipping world is smaller than I thought."

I gave him my papers, and he recorded my signing on.

"This must look like a lifeboat compared to the NBC ore carriers that you've been on," I said after he had put the crew file in the drawer.

He leaned back and put his feet on the desk. "Well, it's like this," he said, "as chief mate with NBC, I made almost double what I'm making here as a captain. But, after I put in one year's service as master on my papers, even if it is on this tub, I can get a captain's job on a real ship making real money."

The steward tapped at the door, then stepped in and put a cup of coffee and a glass of water on the captain's desk, then asked if he would like anything else. "Bring one coffee for the first assistant, and then you can take off," said Captain Petros. He put both hands behind his head and reclined farther. "I've been at the bottom of the ladder too long," he said. "It looks like the people at NBC expect you to be with them at least one hundred years before they'll let you be captain on their ships."

A couple of days later, a chief mate from the island of Kalymnos arrived. During the repair period, at the end of the day, when the weather was nice, the captain, the chief engineer, the chief mate, and I sat under the dockside canopy at midships, having a beer and swapping sea stories. It was usually low tide when that happened, and the ship's deck was on the same level as the deck of the pier. "It's like sitting at a sidewalk café back home," the chief mate had said.

On one of those evenings, not long after we had sat down, three men happened to be walking by on the dock, and when they heard Greek spoken, they stopped to chat. Among the men was Giannis Antoniou, my old classmate and close friend at the Maritime Academy.

We had a spontaneous, warm embrace, and for the first five minutes, we spoke at the same time, bombarding each other with questions.

"I'm still an engine cadet," said Giannis when we managed to get our talking organized. "I was in the Army for two years. I wanted to get that obligation over with, so I went in right after graduation. I'll take the third engineer's exam next month, when I get back."

"Come, let me show you the engine room," I said. "I'm first assistant on this one."

Stepping carefully over piles of loose piping and disassembled machinery, we made the rounds of my engine room's upper and lower platforms. Occasionally, Giannis would make a comment like, "That's what the early Worthington air compressors looked like," or "This must be the first separators De Laval made." He read the serial number on the main engine and asked if Nordberg Diesel was still in business. "I think they have a different name now. Anyway, we have plenty of spare parts," I said.

Later, we went to his ship that was loading grain, two piers over. The main engine, a big six-cylinder Burmeister, was in the middle of his engine room, with plenty of open space around it. Everything was freshly painted, clean, and modern. "Your engine room makes mine look like a cluttered junkyard," I said.

"But you're already first assistant, and I'm still an engine cadet," he answered, then asked me if I had been to Karachi. For many hours after that, we talked about other things, never mentioning the differences between our ships.

It was a pleasant, though brief, reunion. His ship left the next morning for Pakistan.

Giannis was the only classmate and one of the only two graduates from the Maritime Academy that I met abroad during my sailing years. The other one was Filipos Giannakopoulos, the man renting the other room at Sourlis' house in Lamia, whom I met in New York a few months later.

One week before all the repairs were completed, we decided to have the *dock trials* of the main engine. The captain called for a tug and had the ship turned around, where the bow was resting against the solid concrete dock. They put out extra lines forward and aft, and when the mate sent word to me that they were ready, I opened the starting air supply valve. The engine turned slowly, hissing and groaning like a giant waking up after a long slumber. I opened the fuel-supply valve and let it run a couple of revolutions *ahead*, then stopped, and did the same on the *astern* position, while vigilant for any unusual knocking and scraping.

The chief engineer stood on the upper platform, just inside the engine-room casing. "She sounds good," he said after listening for a few minutes, then turned around and went back to his cabin.

Traditionally, the control of the main engine during maneuvering is the domain of the first assistant, and on my previous ships I had only a supporting role in that task. This was the first time I was in complete control of this giant. I moved the throttle up one notch to give it more fuel, and the giant moved faster. Then I moved the handle to *stop*. The giant obeyed immediately. The throttle handle felt like the whip in the hands of a lion tamer commanding a fierce lion to stand on the stool. I moved the handle to the red area of the control mechanism and commanded it to go in reverse. Again, it obeyed. Then I snapped the whip: *faster,* and it submitted; I was the master of this beast!

Right then, I happened to look up and saw a deckhand running down the ladder trying to be heard over the engine noise. "Turning too fast," he shouted when he got closer. "The propeller wash broke the lines of the ship behind us."

I brought the handle to the *stop* position. "The throttle was sticking, but I fixed it," I said.

*

Finally, after two months of banging, cutting, welding, and sticking on Band-Aids, the Nikitas Ship Repair Company declared their work finished. With me keeping a vigilant eye on everything in the engine room and Captain Petros doing the same over the whole ship, we sailed down the Patapsco River into Chesapeake Bay and out into the Atlantic Ocean.

Seven days later, we tied up near the Miami Port Authority on Flagler Avenue, and for two days we had prospective charterers inspecting us. The dock where we were tied up was the same one where the cruise ships docked, but unfortunately, none were there at the time. I would have liked to find out how many of the old acquaintances were still there and visit some of them, especially George Vazeos, the chief engineer of the *Yarmouth Castle*. After chastising me for quitting the *Ariadne*, I wanted him to see me in my new position being in charge of the whole engine room on this ship.

Apparently, none of the prospective charterers found our ship suitable for their needs, and after two days in Miami, we cast off. A day later, we anchored outside Freeport, in Grand Bahama.

In Freeport, we stayed at anchor for a month waiting for orders from headquarters in Texas. Captain Petros and I used that time to fine-tune our ship's performance. Although *Mustang Island* was a small, old ship that belonged to a small, unimportant company, Captain Petros went about his work as if he were in command of the flagship of the Royal Navy. As I was soon to find out, Captain Petros had a big sense of duty and a huge dose of *philotimo*, the Greek word that denotes personal honor and the obligation to do the right thing regardless of the consequences; a virtue that every Greek, supposedly, is born with.

The captain's efforts to bring the old ship into *shipshape* order led to constant disagreements with the office people over his spending. "We need to have some up-to-date navigational instruments and some decent firefighting gear, but they haven't approved any of my requisitions," he told me. "They keep saying everything will be delivered when the ship gets to Galveston, and I told them it'll be a miracle if we make it there."

The waters in Freeport were crystal clear, and the fishing was great. We used to spend most of our non-working time fishing from the ship's stern or from the paint dinghy. One Saturday evening, the captain and I decided to go to the Lucaya Casino for a nice dinner and maybe meet some interesting tourists. We shaved, perfumed, put on our suits, and had the bosun take us ashore in the dinghy. When we got to the Lucaya Casino, we were told that we were early. The restaurant wouldn't be serving dinner for another two hours, but we could spend our time in the casino, the helpful person suggested.

Neither the captain nor I was the gambling type, so we walked around the area to kill time. Everywhere we looked, there were tall pine trees toppled over as if being trampled on by some giant. "That's the footprints of Hurricane Betsy," said Captain Petros. "She came through here last month. I heard she did a lot of damage in South Florida and in the city of New Orleans."

Our walk took us past a boat-rental place, which prompted the captain to suggest we rent a boat and explore the shore. "Need to go back to the ship anyway," he said. "I need to tell the chief mate to ballast Number Five Center. The radio man said earlier had heard there is a weather front forming off the coast of Africa. It could become another Betsy."

After some mild negotiating, we settled on a Boston Waller with an Evinrude engine. "You're sure it has a full tank of gas?" asked the captain before we cast off. "Yes sir, we always provide a full can of fuel. Look," said the rental man and pointed to the red fuel can at the bottom of the boat. Both of us craned our necks and looked at a big F sitting right on the centerline of the sight glass. Neither one of us felt the need to pick up the can and feel the weight.

We went to the ship, and the captain went on board, and I stayed in the boat. Whatever the conversation with the chief mate was, it seemed to have upset him because when he came back, he looked depressed. I asked what was wrong.

"It's nothing; you wouldn't understand anyway. Let's go," he said.

I suggested we go check out a beach around the point. "I heard that's a nudist beach," I said, thinking that would cheer him up. The captain didn't answer. He steered, and I sat on the center bench facing forward, enjoying the feeling of the afternoon breeze on my face. Soon, we rounded the point and lost sight of the ship.

We moved along slowly for a while, then I heard the captain shout, "Hey." I turned, and he nodded his head toward the sun about to disappear below the horizon. The last rays had painted the clouds above bright red, purple, and golden. He made a face that could be interpreted as "pretty" and started humming the song "*La historia de un amor,*" a sure sign his mood was improving.

After a while, we saw the beach and scanned for nudists, but there was nobody in sight, naked or clothed. Then, when we were about five hundred yards from the shore, the engine stopped.

"Did you see something? Why did you stop?" I asked.

"I didn't. It stopped by itself."

Both of us moved to look at the gas can, almost bumping heads. The F was still right in the middle of the sight glass. I shook the can. "It's empty. The damn float is stuck."

At the time there was a strong current that seemed to be moving us away from the shore at a fast rate. We looked around and couldn't see any oars on board or anything else we could use for paddles.

"And it's our luck for the beach to be deserted," I said.

"Damn it, we're going to end up in Cuba," shouted the captain. "We have to do something, let's see if we can push it." We took off our clothes. The captain folded his and placed them on the bow. I dumped mine in a pile at the stern, and we dove into the water. Neither our pushing nor the pulling did any good: we kept getting farther and farther from the beach. We abandoned that idea and got back in the boat.

The boat was made out of molded fiberglass. The only wooden part on board was the bench I had been sitting on. "Let's try to break it and use it as a paddle," the captain said. We both started kicking the bench till we finally broke it loose. Conveniently, it split in half, right down the middle, and we used one piece each as a paddle. We paddled hard and desperately until, half an hour later, we got to where we could stand on the bottom, then we jumped out and pulled the boat on beach. We put our clothes back on, except our jockey shorts, which were wet, and we threw them away. Captain Petros walked to the nearest cottage and used their phone to call the boat-rental place. Soon after, they came and towed us back to the marina.

Later that evening, we had a nice dinner. I don't remember what we ate, but I do remember we had frequent rum-and-Coke toasts for our adventure and to better days. "I wonder if there is anybody else in this fancy place having dinner without underwear on?" said the captain, and we had a hearty laugh. We both agreed it would be nice if we had some company, of the *right kind*, but as we scanned the dining room and lounge areas, the only unescorted women we saw in the place were the waitresses.

"I heard the bosun talk about a love palace on a settlement called West End, not too far from the ship," I said. "Maybe we take a look there after dinner." The captain didn't seem pleased with my suggestion.

"The way I like to do my shore trips," he answered, "is to go to a restaurant with class and have a nice meal, like this. Maybe even see a movie, then go to a hotel and have the woman come to my room. Going to seamen's bars is for the lower classes. Besides, is not good policy for an officer to be swapping whores with the crew, they lose respect for you. When we're done here, we'll walk around the casino area instead, see some regular people, for a change."

And so, we did. We wandered among the gambling tables, and, for a while, we watched people spread fifty and one-hundred-dollar chips on the roulette tables, only to be raked in moments later by the man spinning the wheel.

Then, without warning, the captain suggested we go back to the ship. "Let's get out of here, I'm getting sick," he said.

"We ate the same thing," I said, "I feel fine." He didn't answer.

We walked to the marina and asked one of the men there to take us to the ship. "It'll be five dollars," the man said. When we rounded the point, the ship's silhouette came into view, highlighted by a full moon.

"There she is," said Captain Petros as if talking to himself. Then, "Damn." He slammed his fist against the side of the boat.

"What's the matter?" I asked.

"Life's not fair, that's what's the matter. Did you see that bald guy at the roulette table? The one with a woman glued on either side of him.

He kept covering the table with fifty-dollar chips, and a minute later, when the wheel stopped, they were raked in by the dealer. I bet you in every spin he spent more than I make in six months in this death trap. Damn." Another bang with his fist. "Who decides where a man should be born and what he should be? I'm telling you, Providence up there…" He pointed skywards with the fist-banging hand, "has a twisted sense of humor."

While we were climbing the gangway I was about to suggest having a night cup at the boat-deck and enjoying the full moon but as I was about to open my mouth the captain started cursing his luck again and I thought it would be best to leave him alone.

*

After one month in Freeport, we got orders to sail to Galveston, Texas. While underway, everybody was working in high gear, preparing for the owners who, surely, would be coming on board. Anything made of bronze or copper was rubbed to a sparkle. Cleaning and de-greasing liquids were used in generous quantities, and fresh paint was applied over areas where there was even a suspicion of rust. When it came to cleanliness and shininess, Captain Petros could put any British steward to shame.

We had good weather on the way to Galveston, and Captain Petros was optimistic we would arrive ahead of the time he told the office. The afternoon we were passing by the Florida Keys, I went to the bridge and borrowed their binoculars to look at the fort at the Dry Tortugas. Then on the way to my cabin, I stopped and peeked into the engine room (an instinctive habit). As soon as I opened the door of the engine-room casing, the smell of burning electric insulation hit me, and I dashed down to the engine platform. The motor for the main engine cooling pump was on fire. The engineer on watch stood by, a few feet away, watching the smoke rise and the sparks shoot out, looking totally unconcerned. A few more minutes and the motor would have burned, the pump would quit running, and the main engine would overheat and stop. We would be dead in the water, in the middle of the Gulf. I hustled to put the back-up pump online and isolated the burning motor.

"Why didn't you stop it when you saw the sparks coming out of it?" I shouted to the engineer.

"I thought that's how big motors run. In La Ceiba, the motor for raising the gangway for the launch did that all the time," he answered as calmly as if telling me about some everyday routine, like the time of day, which meant he didn't grasp how big a calamity we had just escaped.

We arrived in Galveston on the afternoon of October twenty. Soon after our arrival, a party atmosphere developed on the ship that lasted for three consecutive days. A steady stream of big-and-tall Texans, with suitably big hats and with wives and children in tow, kept coming and going. The owners, their families, the owners' friends and their families, business associates, company employees, neighbors with their children in tow—the whole town, it seemed—were invited to see the *big boat.* They cautiously climbed the gangway, toured the ship, got impressed by the big engine, had their pictures taken holding the big steering wheel, drank the liquor locker dry, complimented the cook for his excellent appetizers, and left.

When the partying was over, the ship inspectors came in white boiler suits, hard hats, and yellow flashlights. They spent a whole day climbing in and out of the cargo tanks, querying the chief mate and me about pumping capacity and cargo-heating capability, and soon after, we got word that we would be loading a special industrial oil for Naples, Italy.

That announcement gave me cause for some serious thinking. The three months on board had convinced me that a longer stay on the ship would mean, besides hard work, also taking an unnecessary risk. Neither one of the two third assistant engineers under me had any previous sailing experience on a ship of this size. Both had worked on sightseeing boats in La Ceiba, Honduras, and only God knows how they had gotten their Panamanian Engineer's license.

The burning cooling pump motor incident before we arrived in Galveston convinced me that I shouldn't expect much help from my engine crew.

Both third engineers and all three oilers came from the same town in Honduras, and this was the farthest they had been in their sea-going travels. They looked forward to the trip to Europe with child's awe and, unfortunately, with just as much experience.

Sadly, the only support from the chief engineer, a fragile old man who moved about very little and very slowly, was verbal. It had taken me three days to rewind the burned-out motor of the main engine cooling pump, and I had gotten very little help from anyone else from the engine department. Then, when I turned in the overtime, the chief said, very apologetically, that the port engineer thought it was too many hours and had cut it in half. The port engineer didn't want to sign on an electrician with the crew, as was common on most ships of the day, saying it was a small ship and that he was confident I could handle the work myself. The real reason was that he didn't want to pay for it. The whole situation did not make me feel very confident about a long and prosperous career with his company.

Just like Captain Petros, I also wanted the service as first assistant engineer recorded in my papers; it would look good when I tried to get a well-paying job on a bigger and newer ship. On the other hand, it would look bad if the discharge papers said the ship had sunk due to engine failure and, even worse, if I were to go down with her. The prospect of heading towards Italy only to end up drifting in the middle of the Atlantic with a burned-out engine did not appeal to me, and I turned in my resignation before the ship was to start loading.

Captain Petros also had reservations about the ship's ability to survive rough weather in the high seas. After strong disagreements with administrative personnel over filling some of his requisitions for safety equipment, he, too, submitted his resignation. Both of us had come to the conclusion that the Motor Tanker *Mustang Island* was not the ship that would steer our careers in the desired direction.

We left Galveston on November six, 1965. We decided to take a leisure trip to Miami to check out the job prospects there and then plan what to do next. Before boarding the bus in Galveston for New

Orleans, we stopped by the agent's office and picked up our last mail, which had been forwarded there by Mr. Pardalakis.

While the bus was going through the empty plains of Texas, I read my letter from home, and Captain Petros went through his mail. Suddenly, he started cursing.

"What's the matter? Bad news from home?" I asked.

"No, this is a letter from a friend," he said. "He's third mate on board the *Bulker Express*, the ship with the old captain that NBC wanted me to go as chief mate when I saw you in New York, remember?" I told him I remembered.

"He says here that on the way to Venezuela, the old man had a heart attack and was taken to Aruba by helicopter. They put the new chief mate in the captain's position and moved everybody else up a notch. My friend is now second mate on the *Express*. Fucking luck." He banged his fist on the back of the seat in front of us, startling the old black man who was dozing off in it.

"Sorry, the leg slip," I hurried to explain.

"I turned down the *Bulker Express* job because I wanted to put in my papers, time served as captain, and what did I get? Three months on the motor tanker *Mustang Island*, a toy ship that hasn't taken one barrel of cargo yet. I'm telling you: God has a mean sense of humor. Damn." This time, I caught his arm before he hit the seat in front of him.

"Not one ounce of gratitude for all the years of hard work I've given them," he went on. "If that faggot personnel manager at NBC had any *philotimo,* he would have called me to go to Venezuela to take the captain's place," he said.

"Not everybody has as much *philotimo* as you do, Captain," I said.

*

When we arrived in New Orleans, Captain Petros told the cab driver to take us to a hotel with class.

The driver said, "Yes, sir," and took off.

After a while, he parked under a canvas canopy in the middle of the French Quarter. A man, dressed like an admiral, stepped forward and opened our door and said, "Welcome to Château Monteleone."

Another man picked up our battered suitcases and asked us to follow him to the registration. I remember walking into the lobby and feeling like I was entering the hall of some exotic royal palace. Golden chandeliers hung from high ceilings, and large flower arrangements in fancy vases sat on antique tables everywhere. Two curved marble stairways, ascending from opposite sides of the lobby floor, led up to a mezzanine. Everything was big, shining, and regal-looking, and all the people lounging in the lobby dressed as if they were going to a coronation.

After we registered, the porter escorted us to a gleaming elevator operated by an old black man in a starchy blue-and-gold uniform. On the fourth floor, we were escorted to our rooms, and the man asked whether there would be anything else. Captain Petros said he had a pair of pants and a shirt to be pressed, and the man said he'd give them to the room service.

"We're going to the dining room downstairs for a nice dinner later," the captain said. "You should have yours pressed, too."

"I'm okay," I said, "I'll put my pants under the mattress, and I'm going to wear a sweater over my shirt."

We did have a nice dinner that night at the hotel's fancy restaurant, but things didn't work out the way Captain Petros wanted. Instead of cheering up, he got more depressed and repeated a few more times that Providence has a twisted sense of humor. We decided to leave New Orleans and go to Miami the next day, where he had connections and was sure things would be better.

(The reasons that caused the captain with the refined taste to become depressed would make interesting conversation in crews' mess halls and in seamen's bars but would contribute little to the main purpose of this writing, so I'll reserve this part of memory for when I'm swapping stories, if I remember them, with old sea dogs.)

CHAPTER TEN

We thought it would be more fun if we went to Miami by train, and early the next morning, we walked to the station to check the itinerary and get the tickets. As we were leaving the ticket window, a shabby-looking man in old, dirty clothes walked away from a group of scruffy idlers lounging in the corner of the waiting room and approached us. He showed us his badge and said he was with the immigration department and asked if we had just arrived in New Orleans. We told him we bought tickets for the evening train to Miami. He seemed skeptical and asked to see our identification.

"I was hoping I'd get a chance to do this sometime," said the captain. We both pulled out our Greek passports, each with the official American tourist visa stamped on it. (The captain's visa was issued in Venezuela, and mine in Nassau.)

I had heard many horror stories of seamen who jumped ship only to get caught as they were boarding the bus or the train that would take them to the end of their rainbow. In those days, immigration rounded up illegals and shipped them back to their country. They also slapped hefty fines on the companies whose ships they had jumped from and on those who hired them. There were no sanctuary cities and no sympathetic news reporters interviewing troubled illegals. The news hours of the few television stations that existed then were taken up by sports, the Russian threat, the doings of the Kennedys, and the scandalous lives of the movie stars.

I looked with some nervousness at the immigration man's face for expressions of joy or disappointment as he scrutinized our passports. I didn't detect anything, not even an eye twitch, just a bland poker-player's face. He handed us the passports back, said, "Have a nice trip," and returned to being a bum.

It was late in the afternoon when we boarded the train, but there was still enough light to see the landscape and the towns we were going through. The train stopped at a few small towns, most of which seemed to have been named by the local Indians. In a town called Mobile, we stopped for the longest, something about another train coming. Captain Petros told me he had been there before. "Mobile is a big town," he said. "I once stayed for almost a month on drydock with one of the NBC ships. It's not a bad place; that's the kind of town I would like to live in when it's time to swallow the anchor."

"When is time for that?" I asked.

"That's how the British call the staying ashore. How about you? Where would you like to settle?"

"For me," I said, "American towns may be interesting to visit, but for permanent living, I would like to find a little town by the sea somewhere in the south of England." (As I write this, a train, blowing a long, annoying whistle, is passing by. My place of business is next to the railroad track, only a few hundred yards away from the station in Mobile, Alabama, where I had the conversation with Captain Petros on that November day a long time ago. Funny how life turns out.)

We arrived in Miami on Thursday afternoon on the eleventh of November 1965. Sticking to the captain's plan, we got separate rooms at the Castaways Inn, in Miami Beach: a classy place in a classy neighborhood. After a brief rest, we headed to Little Havana on Eighth Street. Both of us had been there before, and with the captain speaking Spanish fluently, it was a place where we could get the most for our money.

That night, we dined at a restaurant that had white tablecloths and snooty waiters. After dinner, we went to a nightclub next door. It had a Latin-American band, and the captain said it was frequented by locals. It didn't take us long to get paired with two curvy beauties who swore they had fallen in love with us the moment we walked through the door. We knew they were *business girls*, but they were dressed and behaved like they were secretaries in an office. It was a pleasant evening and progressed into a pleasant night.

The next day, after the obligatory touristy things—late breakfast, walk on the legendary Miami Beach to ogle at the bikinis, lunch by the seaside, and have a noon nap—we were ready for a repeat of the previous day's activities. It was Friday, the departing day for the cruise ships, so, on our way to Little Havana, we stopped and watched the *Ariadne*, my old ship, as she was going out of Miami Ship Channel, followed by the *Bahama Star*. The *Florida* was getting ready to depart. A band played "Anchors Away," the passengers tooted horns and threw streamers, and the line handlers were casting off the mooring lines.

The last of the cruise ships, *Yarmouth Castle,* was still loading. George Vazeos, her chief engineer, was on the dock fussing at the two men taking on the engine stores. We walked over and greeted him. It didn't take long after I said "Hi" for George to start his chastising sermon about squandering my savings and wasting the best years of my life. "I told you I'll be back," I said when he paused for a breath. "Do you need a second engineer?"

"You got perfect timing," he said. "One of the Thirds had to rush home; his father got sick. I was going to call Pardalakis as soon as I was done with the stores."

"I have the second engineer's license now," I said. "I was first assistant on the last ship. If I go to New York, I'm sure Pardalakis will find me a First's position with no problem."

"And what good will that do you? You'll squander it anyway. If you come on board now as Third, you can have the Second's job when he goes home in two months."

"Sounds good," I said. "But I need a couple of weeks of vacation. I just got off a ship where I had to work my butt off. I'll come on the second trip. Is it okay?"

That request seemed to reignite his lecture-fire about squandering my money and about regretting it when I got to be his age. "I'll tell you this," he concluded. "I'll manage this trip shorthanded, but if you want the job, be here," he gestured with his finger, almost touching the dock he stood on, "when we get back from Nassau next week, or I'm calling Pardalakis to send me an engineer."

I told him I would be there, and I truly meant it.

"And if you want," George said to Captain Petros, "you can go talk to the captain," he pointed upward with his finger. "He's Greek too, and I hear the staff captain is going on vacation next month."

Captain Petros said he might do that on the next trip. We wished George a "good trip" and slowly we walked forward for Captain Petros to have a better look at the old-fashion wheelhouse. "It looks to be all teak and mahogany, you don't see any like that anymore," he said.

By the time we turned around, Vazeos had finished taking his supplies, the gangway was up and the band on the upper deck was playing "Anchors Away". People were lined up on the dockside of the ship's decks tossing streamers and confetti to those waving on the dock.

We got into a taxi and headed for our rendezvous at Calle Ocho.

*

It was another fun evening in Little Havana, and late into the night, we returned to the comfort of the Castaways Inn, tired and sleepy. I was sound asleep before I even touched the bed—perhaps the result of too many *Cuba Libres*.

The persistent ringing of the telephone awakened me. When I finally answered it, Captain Petros, sounding unusually excited, told me to turn on my television. I staggered up to it and turned the knob. Immediately, the screen filled with a picture of a ship in flames. My half-asleep brain thought it was an old movie with pirate ships battling in the high seas, which Captain Petros knew I liked to watch, but tonight, all I wanted was to continue my sleep. I mumbled some unkind things about the captain's taste and reached to turn it off, but just as I touched the knob, the announcer said the ship's name, and my hand froze. I looked closer and there she was—the *Yarmouth Castle* turned into a huge fireball. All the sleepiness disappeared in an instant, and I sat cross-legged on the bed staring at the television set, unflinching.

I had heard many stories of shipwrecks and of ships torpedoed by the Germans and sent to the bottom. Almost every old-timer in the ships I had been on had a large inventory of disaster stories, all of which—appropriately embellished when recounted in mess halls and poop decks during long, calm passages—had happened in stormy seas where the storytellers had to swim in frigid waters, battle starving sharks and lifeboat-swallowing waves, and drift in the ocean for days before they were rescued. But this was the first time I had witnessed a real ship disaster happening almost in front of me, and to people I had spoken with just hours earlier.

After a few minutes, I put on my clothes and went over to Captain Petros' room. We sat at the edge of the bed and, stunned, watched as dazed passengers in their pajamas plunged into the sea. Every so often, we could see a Coast Guard helicopter and parts of the tail of another that we assumed was from the television station. They kept circling the *Castle* and occasionally would show another passenger ship, the *Bahama Star*, and a freighter standing further away, both surrounded by lifeboats. We kept staring at the television, and from time to time one of us would whisper, "Isn't that something?" Only hours earlier, those same people now getting fished out of the water, scorched and half-drowned, had been throwing streamers, blowing kisses, and dancing on the deck.

At first light, I rushed to the corner newsstand and bought the *Miami Herald*. The Sunday edition was full of pages of advertisements and movie star news, making it hard to find what I was looking for. I kept the news section and handed the bundles of glossy pages with the car photographs and grocery store coupons back to the man.

"Take this back," I said. "Too much paper."

"For you, it probably *is* too much paper," answered the smart-mouthed guy, and for an instant, I felt like punching him.

Back in the room, Captain Petros and I dissected the paper. A two-page section that seemed to have been added at the last minute included many photographs showing the ship listing at an angle, about to roll over, with flames pouring from every porthole. Other photographs showed people in orange life jackets jumping over the side and people bobbing in the water, their hands raised and their mouths open. I realized that I had come very close to being one of those half-singed people bobbing in the water myself, and silently I thanked the angel saddled with my protection.

"From what I understand, the person who wrote this news doesn't have anything good to say about the Greek captain," I said.

"To the blabbermouth reporters, sitting warm and comfortable behind an office desk, saying what the captain should or shouldn't have done at that moment comes easy," Captain Petros answered.

We wondered what happened to George Vazeos and the other Greeks on board. Captain Petros and I went to the docks and asked around, but we couldn't get any accurate information from anybody. In later issues of the newspaper, we learned that 87 people were lost, including two crew members: the ship's doctor and a stewardess. Each died helping the passengers, the paper said.

For the rest of the time we were in Miami, the television stations kept showing, almost constantly, interviews with the survivors and the crew members of *Yarmouth Castle* and the *Bahama Star*. Through it all, the captain and the rest of the Greeks on the *Castle* did not come out looking good. It was not a bright moment for the Greek mariners. (Much later, I worked with George Vazeos, but whenever I started talking about the sinking, he would say he didn't want to talk about it and either change the subject or walk away. I had heard from others that his performance and that of the other Greeks during that tragedy was not the kind that would make our heroic ancestors proud.)

Two days later, Captain Petros and I decided to ride the train from Miami to New York and try our luck at finding a ship there. By now, the city should have been familiar territory to me, yet I still managed to get lost every time I went farther than the two blocks from the hotel where I was staying. (An imperfection that has haunted me all my life and had prompted my wife to comment on many occasions when we traveled together, that it was a good thing I became an engineer instead of a captain.)

A few days after arriving to New York, while returning from Greenwich Village to my room at the Rex Hotel, in the early hours of the morning, I boarded the wrong subway train and ended up in Washington Heights. When I discovered the mistake, I headed for the lower platform to get on the right train, and there, who do I see coming up the stairs but Philipas Gianacopoulos, the fellow who was renting the room next to mine at the Surlis' house during my first three years at the Maritime Academy, in Lamia.. He had jumped ship a year earlier and got a job in a piano-making factory. He was working the second shift and was on his way home.

We had a joyous reunion and stayed up way past sunrise, catching up on each other's news. Someone from his village had arranged for him to marry a Puerto Rican for the green card, he said. He had paid her five hundred dollars for the deal. He would pay another five when the divorce was finalized in a month.

Again, just as he did during our years at the Maritime Academy in Lamia, when we were roommates, he served as my guide in New York. He took me to nice restaurants, to church, and to a dance given by the Greek community. The Sunday I attended church services, they passed a special tray to raise money for the campaign of a Greek man named Spiro Agnew, who was running for governor of Maryland.

*

Soon after, I signed on as third engineer on board the *Gypsum Duchess*, an ore carrier owned by US Gypsum. Before I left, Philipas gave me his massive, 1943, *Modern Marine Engineer's Manual*, the bible of all marine engineers at the time.

"I won't need it anymore," he said. I still have it. Sometimes I leaf through it, looking at drawings of propulsion diesel engines made by DOXFORD, NORBDERG, and FAIRBANKS MORSE. It reminds me of what a struggle it was changing the pistons and cleaning the scavenge-air chamber, and I feel envious of the new generation of engineers.

Sadly, through mostly my fault, I didn't keep in touch with Philipas. Sometimes I wonder where he may be these days.

I think Captain Petros returned to National Bulk Carriers. I didn't see him anymore after that time, and, regrettably, I forgot his last name, so I cannot Google him.

My new ship was a self-unloading ore carrier that transported material used to make sheetrock, a relatively new product widely used in the construction of new buildings. The two most frequent ports we loaded from were Hantsport, Nova Scotia, and Ocho Rios, Jamaica.

Then we would unload at the US Gypsum plants on the Gulf and East Coasts of the U.S. Our loading in Hantsport used a hummingbird-style approach. We had to dash in during the incoming tide, load, and get out before the low tide; otherwise, we would end up sitting at the bottom.

In Ocho Rios, we stayed much longer because it was a small loading facility. Having been there many times before, when I was on the *Ariadne,* I was familiar with the town and acted as a guide to the men on my watch. A few times while loading, I saw a small American Navy tanker taking on water at the adjacent pier. The chief mate said that from time to time, when Castro got pissed off at the Americans or wanted to squeeze a favor out of them, he would cut the water supply to the Guantanamo base in Cuba.

My ship had steam turbines for propulsion, mostly Canadians for crew, and mostly Brits for officers. She was well-kept, the food was to my liking, the work easy, and the money good. Also, the ports-of-call were interesting, although none would match the staying time of my first ship, the good-old *Maritihi.*

My coworkers and the rest of the crew seemed like nice people, also. The only time I got into any type of disagreement with the chief engineer was when he chastised me for having a beer at a tavern in Ocho Rios with the fireman of my watch, a man from Bombay doing a stint as a fireman while working on his master's degree in philosophy at the University of Halifax.

"An officer is not supposed to fraternize with the crew," he told me.

I said "Okay," barely resisting the urge to tell him that on the previous trip, it was that fireman and my oiler who hauled his smashed Excellency on board, barely a minute before the deckhands raised the gangway.

It seemed that alcohol was one thing the Brits and Canadians had low tolerance for, and the ship's rules were strict about having any liquor in the cabin. There were no *rum rations* I had read in novels, nor bottled beer as was issued at the Greek ships with dinner on holidays. The only time I saw any alcohol served on board was during the

Christmas holiday in the form of rum pudding. Most of the men got second helpings of the putting while complaining that the cook had skimped on the rum.

I planned to stay on board for a while, but because of their lopsided vacation rules, I ended up staying only two months. The man I replaced had slipped on the oily floor in the boiler room, broken his leg, and was taken to the hospital. Had it not been for his accident, he would have gone on vacation in January.

"His replacement is scheduled to report on board in Hantsport," the chief engineer told me. "The main office should have made that clear to you when you were hired. I apologize. I'm putting in a good report for you, and I'm sure they'll be calling you soon to go to one of their other ships." So, on the twenty-first of January 1966, I was back in New York, at the Hotel Rex on Forty-Seventh Street.

Sometimes, I wonder how different my life would have turned out had the fireman of the *Gypsum Duchess* been more careful and not spilled the oil on the boiler room floor, or that engineer been more careful where he was stepping.

The first thing I did after getting a room at the Rex Hotel was to go by the Gypsum Company office. The personnel man wrote down the address and phone number of where I was staying and said he had been instructed to include my name on the engine-room crew's list for engineers on the *Gypsum Empress*. "She will be coming to New Jersey in two weeks, or so. I'll be calling you," he said.

*

With my next job secured, I joined a few others between-ship mariners staying at the hotel and proceeded to play tourist. Most of us, in order to save money, would frequently have lunch at the *Automat*, a strange American invention of an automatic restaurant, one block away from the hotel. It was one big room with shelves along the three walls serving as tables, and also a place to keep the ketchup, mustard, and relish bottles. The fourth wall of the room was lined with small cupboards with glass doors, through which you could see the different sandwiches stored inside. If you put the right number of coins in the slot next to the door, the door would open, and you could get the sandwich. (Somebody behind that wall would replenish it soon after.)

One day, I couldn't find the ketchup for my hot dog, and I called through the cupboard door and asked for it from face with a thick mustache that appeared at the opening.

"We stopped putting it out; the hobos put it in hot water and make tomato soup," explained the face, then handed me two packets of ketchup through the cupboard.

If we wanted something with Greek flavor for dinner, we would go to Molfetas's Restaurant on Forty-Eighth and Broadway.

Some of the sightseeing activities included occasional trips to Greek nightclubs, the *bouzoukia*, as we called them, to hear Greek music and watch the belly-dancers. Also, trips to Greenwich Village to gawk at the gays and lesbians—they were a rarity in those days—and to Radio City to watch the Christmas Spectacular, mainly the bare-legged Rockettes. We also spent a lot of time by the Rockefeller Plaza, admiring the huge Christmas tree and the shapely, limber skaters at the rink below. They seemed to glide so gracefully and effortlessly on the ice surface as if there was nothing to it.

In Central Park, there was a lake that froze over in winter and was used for public ice skating by people with average skating skills and less show-offish tendencies than the Rockefeller Plaza skaters.

One day, five of us, after watching those in the rink for a while, convinced ourselves we could do it also. We rented the skates and got among the crowd gliding in circles on the ice. It was a disaster. In the few seconds we managed to stay upright, we gave everyone around us a deathly scare. We were about to give up when someone in the group—it must have been a captain—came up with a suggestion: "Why don't all five of us form a circle and lock arms? That way, we get a larger support surface, and if one slips, the others will hold him up." It sounded like a good idea until we tried it. Looking back now, we were lucky we left that place without any broken limbs and without sending to the hospital any of those couples or their children who were innocently gliding in circles. We were like an oversized human cannonball rolling loose on the slippery surface, bouncing from side to side, crashing into everything, and knocking everybody down. It took only a few minutes for the skating rink attendants to dash in, untangle us, and escort us gently, but firmly, out of harm's way.

(Many years later, at the coaxing of my three adorable daughters and a persuasive wife, I found myself gliding along the wall of the skating rink at Ober Gatlinburg, in Tennessee, firmly holding on to the rail and promising to catch up with them shortly.)

Our Central Park adventure, embellished every time it was repeated by the idlers at the seamen's union office, provided entertainment at our expense for a long time. For a while, when one of us, the adventurous five, entered Pardalakis' office, they were hailed as the king of the ice rinks, followed by a laughing narration of how we earned that title.

CHAPTER TEN

The day destined to determine the rest of my life started like all my other vacation days at the time. It was in early February of 1966, a few days after the ice-skating venture. Snow seemed to fall every night, and the locals said it was an unusually heavy winter for New York. I had signed off the bulk carrier *Gypsum Duchess* two weeks earlier and was waiting for the *Gypsum Empress* to arrive in New Jersey, where I was to sign on as a second engineer. I woke up around noon, still sore from the crazy ice-skating attempt in Central Park and walked to the minuscule Parthenon luncheonette next to the Hotel Rex. I ordered the day's special, meatloaf a-la-Kosta (which, I'm sure it consisted of everything left over from the day before), and tried to think what I was going to do the rest of the day.

I was the only customer in the place at the time, and while I was eating, Kostas, the proprietor, came over to chat with me. When I finished with the meatloaf and the conversation, I walked the few blocks to Broadway and Forty-Eighth Street, to the Greek cinema. They were showing a new movie with some popular Greek actors, and those who had seen it said it was very good. On the way, I slipped on the sidewalk and, while trying to avoid falling into a mound of dirty snow, my right foot landed in a puddle, and my shoe filled with ice-cold water. Bad omen, *it's going to be a lousy day.*

When I got to the cinema, the man at the ticket booth informed me that the movie was almost half over. "It's a detective movie, they're more interesting if you see it from the beginning," he said. "It'll be restarting in an hour."

I told him I would be back in an hour, and I went across the street, on the second floor, where the union office of Greek Merchant Seamen was.

Walking in, I got the usual greeting, "Here comes the ice champ," from one of the four guys lounging on the two sofas. I ignored him.

I said, "Good morning," to Mr. Pardalakis, who looked up from writing to return the greeting and ask me how I managed to get the last batch of Jamaican stamps I had brought him. I told him there was a Jamaican engine-room wiper on the ship whose brother worked for the post office in Kingston.

"That's some good stuff," he said. "Thank you."

I poured myself a cup of coffee, sat on the couch, and took off my shoes. I was in the middle of drying my feet when the phone rang. From the joking tone of the one-sided dialogue I could hear, I guessed Mr. Pardalakis was speaking with someone in a warm and sunny place. Then I heard him tell the caller: "No, I haven't had any engineers come by asking for work. Our friend, Theodoros Pitsios, is here, but he's not looking; he's on vacation. Yeah, sure. Just a minute. Theodoros," he called, "George Vazeos wants to talk to you." Holding the wet sock in one hand, I limped over to his desk and took the receiver.

The conversation lasted about two minutes. The first minute was a repeat of previous lectures about wasting my youth, squandering my money, and regretting it when I get to be his age, if I was lucky. (It used to annoy me when older people preached that sermon to me, but now, quite often, I catch myself lecturing the same thing to my grandchildren. It must be something that comes with old age, like arthritis and constipation.)

When the lecture was over, he said he needed an engineer to work with him on a freighter that got blown onto the beach by Hurricane Betsy. "She's set right in front of a big hotel near Palm Beach. Women in skimpy bathing suits are running all over the place, some of them diving right off the stern of the ship. Want to come?"

I think I got to LaGuardia Airport before he even hung up. On the plane, I gazed out the window and saw the city of New York below covered in snow. The radio in the taxi had said that it was going to be another freezing day. I was heading to where women in skimpy bathing suits were diving from the stern of my ship. My guardian angel was on the ball!

Vazeos met me at the airport in Miami and drove me in his Cadillac to where the ship was beached. On the way he briefed me about the work. "She's a Canadian-built, Liberty-class ship that was owned by some Greek," he said. "She ran aground at Singer Island, the night of the hurricane Betsy. Her name is *Amaryllis*. The insurance declared her a *total loss,* and an American named Sam McIntosh from Miami bought her. Right now, the cargo rates are pretty high, and he's planning to operate her when she's off the reef."

The Amaryllis on the beach of Singer Island, 1965

"How did they find you?" I asked.

"McIntosh hired an Austrian salvage master to refloat her. He plans to put two anchors out, then raise steam and pull her off the reef with the ship's winches. When he went on board and saw that all the instruction manuals, valve labels, and signs on the machinery were in Greek, he told McIntosh they needed to hire a Greek engineer. The ship's agent called me, and I went over and talked to them. You see, Sam McIntosh is a dealer for used aviation equipment. To the eyes of someone outside this business, dragging a ship off the reef seems easy.

But after I had a look at her, I told them: I guarantee you, there is not going to be anything easy about it. To get the machinery ready for the big pull, I'll need one, maybe two more engineers. There is going to be a lot of strain on those winches, and we don't know what shape they are in, probably we'll have to rebuild them completely.' They said "okay" and that's when I called Pardalakis."

Vazeos said I could have the chief engineer's cabin; he would be sleeping at his house in Miami. After I got settled, I did some exploring around the chief's office and, judging from the notes I found in his desk drawers, the ship was in bad shape. She was on her way to the Jacksonville Shipyard for repairs; the repair list I found was thicker than the New York phone book. Doing all that work would probably cost the owners more than the ship was worth. Hurricane Betsy was a godsend to them.

Reading through the engine log, it appeared that the captain had done everything by the book. He had recorded in his log that the pipe supplying steam to the steering engine had ruptured, and they couldn't use the rudder. When the captain saw that the ship was heading toward the beach, he dropped both anchors, but the water must have been too deep because both chains broke off the holding pad-eyes at the bottom of the chain locker and were lost. The ship went over a coral reef and came to rest in front of the swimming pool of the Rutledge Motel. After the storm, every time there was a high tide, the captain would run the engine at *Full Astern*, even though the lowest blade of the propeller was about twelve inches above the water, so he could record in the ship's log that he tried to get off the reef.

I found out later that when the insurance people finished investigating, and the ship was declared a total loss, the enterprising captain negotiated with a local scrap dealer for the sale of some nonferrous material from the ship, including the three rows of one-inch-thick degaussing copper cable running alongside the port and starboard sides. I'm sure somewhere in Greece, there is a country villa paid for by the profits of that little transaction.

The plan, the salvage master presented to Sam McIntosh, was to place two anchors a few hundred yards away from the stern and, at high tide when the weather was right, heave on them with the ship's steam winches and drag her over the reef and into deep water. Then, once she was afloat, all she needed was to paint the owner's insignia on the smokestack and sail the seven seas.

It seems that Sam McIntosh had strange notions about cost savings. He insisted, despite the salvage master's objections, on trying to locate and retrieve the old ship's anchors, the ones the captain had dropped during the hurricane to keep the ship from running into the beach. He and a diver spent weeks searching for them up and down the coast instead of buying a pair of replacement anchors from a scrapyard.

My job was to make sure the boilers could raise the steam needed and the winches were in top condition to do the heavy pulling when the time came. George Vazeos and I spent our time getting the boilers operational and the winches in top shape. The main engine and the auxiliary machinery were similar to my first ship, and it was like being on the good-old *Maritihi* once again, only George was nothing like Mastro Pandelis.

I soon learned that in any marine salvage operation, there is a lot of waiting: waiting for the equipment to arrive, waiting for the weather to be right, waiting for the tide. Lots of waiting. And the refloating operation of the *Amaryllis* was no exception.

In the early days of the salvage operation, we had a full deck crew on board, including a cook and a steward, as if the ship would be leaving port the next day. When the workday was over, most of us sat on the hatch covers and watched the people on the beach and the surfers in dark rubber suits, while some deckhand's radio blared, "These boots are made for walking," or "Stop in the name of love," or some other song of the day.

The surfers, mostly guys, would lie face down on their boards and paddle back and forth, staying close to the beach, but there were a few of them who would go a couple of hundred yards out, then stand on their board and sail on top of the wave crest all the way to the shore. It was the first time I had seen this surfing game, and I didn't know what to make of it. It looked like a challenging thing and, apparently, it took some skill to do it, but in my way of thinking, I couldn't see a purpose in all that effort. In the village where I grew up, every effort exerted was to accomplish a goal: feed the goats, hoe the garden, pick the olives. Even the games we played had a defined purpose: to score more points and beat the opponent. Surfing seemed to demand a lot of work for the puny thrill of riding the wave crest for a few seconds.

George Vazeos bought a primitive version of a Beach Buggy, and we used to ride in it up and down the beach. It was an old Army Jeep with broad tires and a noisy engine that lasted about two weeks. Then the engine started knocking badly, and when he took it to the shop, he found out that those who sold it to him had put sawdust in the transmission and in the engine sump. He ended up selling it to a scrap yard.

The salvage master's name was Clemens Brandle. He was from Austria. He had spent some time in Greece and knew the area where I grew up. He was an ex-air force pilot, around forty years old, who had lived in England and Morocco, had transported Cubans during the Mariel boatlift, and spoke five or six languages—a real Indiana Jones type.

We soon became good friends, and sometimes we went for long drives in his long, shiny Chevrolet Impala, or visited the local pubs. Some evenings we went to a lounge called *The Schooner,* where a man played the piano and did some kind of show. Clemens met a woman there named Verdi, a divorcée with a cheerful personality who used to spend the evening chatting with the barmaid while sipping on a large glass of Coca-Cola. I guess Verdi felt sorry for me sipping my drink alone while she laughed her head off at Clemens' jokes because one evening, a bit over a month after I joined the *Amaryllis*, she had us over to her house for dinner and introduced me to Dorothy, one of her nieces.

Dorothy was a sweet and beautiful girl, but madly in love with a guy named Bill who, at the time, was in the Air Force serving in

Vietnam. After a couple of dates, dull for both of us, she must have told her aunt that I was getting on her nerves, because one evening Verdi invited us to another dinner at her house and, instead of Dorothy, there was another niece: Brenda.

One of my regrets now, at this late point in my life, is that I haven't kept a journal. Apart from a few scribblings on daily planners about meeting schedules and luncheon appointments when I got into business, I have no written record of any major event of my life. If I had kept a diary, that dinner at Verdi's house would've been written in bold, capital letters.

Brenda was in her senior year of high school, had a stunning figure, a cheerful personality, and a smile that could unlock the gates of even the fiercest-guarded castle. After dinner, she told me that she had written a term paper on *Mutiny on the Bounty* as a senior project. She asked me whether Clemens, who held the rank of captain, was anything like Captain Bligh and whether I was as rebellious as Fletcher Christian. I told her Christian was a deck officer and I was an engineer.

"Engineers are the kind of people who think things carefully," I said. "They are calmer, they're ..." I was trying to think of how to say *less impetuous* in English.

"Boring?" Brenda interjected with a chuckle.

"No, not boring, more ... accurate, more practical," I protested.

We had been sitting on the couch trying to watch a show titled "I Spy" on the television. I don't think I glanced at the set more than once; I was too busy watching Brenda's face. I was captivated by her spontaneous laughter and her cute gestures as she tried to explain to me what the show was about. I could have sat there for the rest of the night, watching her.

*

By the time Mr. Sam McIntosh decided to buy two anchors and put them in place, a couple of big storms had pushed the ship farther up on the reef. When we finally pulled on the anchors during the highest tide and heaviest swell, no matter how hard the winches strained, the ship wouldn't budge.

By then, the *Amaryllis* had become the darling of the local newspaper and the television channel. Almost every day, television cameras and reporters were recording the comings and goings of the salvage crew. And there was always a steady flow of tourists; some were content to be photographed pretending to be pushing the ship off the beach, but others would climb aboard for a closer look, and some would even attempt to carry something away as a souvenir. Captain Brandle had to assign a full-time guard to the gangway to keep visitors away.

There was no shortage of suggestions as to what the salvage master should do to get *the big boat* off the beach. People wrote to the newspaper or called the radio station and, after voicing their frustration with our inability to solve such a simple problem, outlined their suggestions. Captain Brandle, whose English was perfect, would read for us or tell us about them, and we would have a hearty laugh.

I still remember a couple of those suggestions. One was to fill all cargo holds with water and let it sit for two weeks so the weight would push the reef down, then pump out the water, and the ship would float away. The other was to tie lots of blimp-size balloons on the ship and, during a full moon, fill them with helium. We should make sure, the person suggested, to have a tugboat pulling the ship out to sea to prevent the wind from carrying her farther inland. "You don't want the *Amaryllis* to land on top of city hall," we were cautioned.

But, after a while, the suggestions stopped being funny, and real complaints started coming in. The smoke from the boilers bothered the hotel customers, the noise of the machinery was too loud, and the ship's crew was rowdy. When was the ship going to go away?

After multiple futile attempts to pull the ship off the reef, Mr. McIntosh decided to scrap her. The scrapping would be done in stages, starting with high-value items such as the propeller, propeller shafts, and deck copper piping. These items would be stored in the Number Four cargo hold using the ship's winches, and when ready, loaded onto a barge and taken to the scrapyard. I was glad they had decided to do things that way; it meant I was needed to make sure the boilers and the winches were kept in good operating condition.

Once the decision to scrap her was made, I started burning in the boilers the wood from the cabin paneling and anything else flammable, which, at times when the wind was blowing from the wrong direction, prompted protesting phone calls from the manager of the Rutledge Motel. (The wooden hatch covers were sold to someone who was going to make table-tops out of them.)

At Brenda's suggestion, I enrolled in a driver's school and, after some effort, managed to get my driver's license. I rented a Mustang convertible, and we would take short trips with her cousin, Cyrese, and her boyfriend, Jim Colbert. It was the first time I had a close-up look at the way Americans live and entertain themselves.

One Saturday, when Jim's parents were out of town for the weekend, he invited us to his house to grill steaks. When Brenda started making the salad, she thought we needed more lettuce, and I volunteered to go to the grocery store down the street.

"Get the head kind," she said. "It's cheaper." Perhaps because, until then, the only kind of lettuce I had known was what the Americans call romaine, I brought back a head of cabbage instead of *the head kind* of lettuce, and that gave Jim Colbert a good laugh.

"I thought you grew up on a farm, can't you tell the difference between cabbage and lettuce?" I felt my ears getting hot.

"I will go to return it," I mumbled, but as I started out, Brenda stopped me.

"I'm glad you got it," she said, "I was planning on making coleslaw. You saved me the trip. Coleslaw goes better with steak, and we have enough salad anyway."

During dinner, I noticed Brenda ate very little of the salad and much more of the coleslaw. It was much later, when I ran the whole incident through my head again, that I grasped the full meaning of her gesture.

*

Captain Clemens began having strong differences of opinion with the owner and with a man named Mike Zambetis, a fast-talking Greek, whom the owner had contracted to dispose of the material removed from the ship. When he found out a construction company was doing a big job in the Bahamas and was looking for people with experience in handling and maintaining marine equipment, Clemens made an appointment for an interview. He asked me if I wanted to go along, and I did. The interviewer first talked to us about his company. Frederick Snare Corporation, he said, was an old, family-owned New York-based corporation that had done major construction projects all over the world.

He said the Bahamas' job consisted of improving the port of Nassau: constructing a new breakwater, dredging the harbor, and building a new pier to accommodate larger cruise ships. It also included creating an artificial island from dredge spoils and constructing a bridge connecting Nassau with Paradise Island. The job was expected to last about two years, he said.

Frederic Snare hired Clemens as the marine superintendent in Nassau, and two weeks later, he sent word for me to join the company as a maintenance mechanic on their marine equipment, which included a fleet of five steam-driven floating cranes. As I remember, my pay was four hundred a week plus overtime, a fortune at the time. I was on top of the world. I said goodbye to Brenda and promised to come visit every chance I got.

I had been on board the *Amaryllis* for three months.

Brenda discovered that her family had some distant relatives living in Nassau and convinced her mother that it would be proper to rekindle the old family ties. She came to Nassau a week after I got there and stayed for the long weekend. She even visited one of the uncles while there. After that, she came over every time she could get away.

Maybe here is a good place to say something about Brenda's Bahamian relatives. Those relatives were second and third-generation uncles and cousins, remnants from the migration of the Crown Loyalists of the American Revolution. Both of her grandparents were born in the Bahamas, and later, like many other loyalists who had moved there, returned to the United States. In the late sixties, after Fidel Castro's revolution diverted the tourist trade from Cuba to the Bahamas, many of those who had left came back to reclaim their ancestral land, which had skyrocketed in value. Brenda's grandparents opted not to bother with their properties in Long Island and Eleuthera, preferring to leave them to the squatters. There is a book called *The Winds from the Carolinas,* by Robert Wilder, that, if one substituted some of the protagonists' names with those of Brenda's ancestors, would give a fairly accurate picture of their early life on the islands.

In Nassau, the relatives she saw most often were an uncle (who owned a garage and gas station) and his son, a pilot for Bahamasair with a nice house on the outskirts of town.

In none of my grandiose plans about my future was there a provision about me getting married and settling in South Florida. When the time to settle down came, which I envisioned in the very, very distant future, it would probably be in a country cottage in a pastoral setting somewhere in South England—I was deep into Dickens and Cronin at the time. When daydreaming, I pictured myself strolling the British countryside, gazing at the European continent from the white cliffs of Dover. If not England, France was my second choice. (I still remembered some of the French Mr. Kambanaris taught in high school). America was never under consideration. It was a big country with lots of beautiful scenery, but I thought it lacked the coziness and finesse of Europe. But, as I said, all of that was at retirement, and retirement was far, far away; I was going to see the world first.

All these far-reaching-into-the-future thoughts disappeared when Brenda made her appearance. I proposed to her on her fourth visit to the island, while walking along the Nassau wharf one balmy afternoon. We kissed, and holding hands, we walked to the first jewelry shop we came upon on Bay Street, and she picked up a thirty-dollar engagement ring.

Brenda's High School Graduation Picture - 1966

My sailing days were over.

Looking back now, I think that was the wisest decision I ever made.

THE END

EPILOGUE

Thanassis Grammatikos, myself, and Giannis Antoniou in retirement

Many years later, through the efforts of Thanassis Gramatikos, the four of us, friends from the Maritime Academy, now retired from the sea, came together again. We talked of the *good old days*, swapped sea stories, listed our aches and pains, and compared wrinkles. Mitsaras had cancer. Although at the time of our get-together, he looked well and assured us he felt great, he died a few months later.

Giannis Antoniou delved into farming after retirement. He planted a vineyard, and every year he made wine from his harvest, which he bottled, labeled *Ktima Mastroyannis*, and gave it out as gifts. He also had a vegetable garden with a variety of tomatoes and other vegetables. Always the meticulous, orderly engineer, he had installed an irrigation system with a timer and flow control so each plant would get the right amount of water at the right time. On our first visit, he showed me around his place. His garden shed, his cellar, and all his workstations were spotless, and all the tools were mounted on pegboard by size and service. I made the mistake of letting Brenda come along. When we were leaving his place Brenda half seriously, half-jokingly commented: "You said you were friends for four years, none of that neatness rubbed off on you, did it?"

Thanassis retired in Athens but spent a lot of time in his village, where he started a quarterly newspaper called *The Kastelia News*. He had married a schoolteacher, a delightful lady who died of cancer in 2012.

On my trip to Greece in the fall of 2018, Thanassis and I spent a day in Lamia. We visited the old hangouts and reminisced about our years at the academy. In the evening, before calling it a day, we stopped for a nightcap at one of the coffee shops that had tables spread out at the *Platia Eleutherias* (Freedom Square). Soon after we sat down, the table next to us got occupied by a group of three middle-aged couples already engaged in a heated discussion about the upcoming elections. Everyone in the group seemed to have strong preferences and opinions about the candidates running. Thanassis glanced at them for a moment, then seemed to spend some time looking at the balcony of the building across the square.

"What are you thinking?" I asked.

"It was on that balcony that Karamanlis made a speech when he was running for re-election in May of 1958. We were standing over that corner cheering, do you remember?"

"It seems like yesterday," I said.

He took another glance at the next table. The political debate was still going on. "I just realized," he said, turning to face me, "none of these people was born when we were doing that."

"Thanassis, we're old," I said.

He took a slow sip of his drink while staring at the balcony. "Like you said, it seems like yesterday," he said.

Thanassis died in January 2019 of a heart attack.

www.ingramcontent.com/pod-product-compliance
Lightning Source LLC
LaVergne TN
LVHW051000080826
845145LV00009B/2374

* 9 7 8 1 9 4 2 1 8 1 5 8 3 *